The Guidance of the Holy Spirit

Rev. Dr. Jackson Yenn-Batah

The Guidance of the Holy Spirit

Copyright © 2023 by Rev. Dr. Jackson Yenn-Batah

Paperback ISBN: 978-1-63812-639-3
Ebook ISBN: 978-1-63812-642-3

All rights reserved. No part in this book may be produced and transmitted in any form or by any means, electronic, or mechanical, including photocopying, recording, or by any information storage and retrieval system, without permission in writing from the copyright owner.

The views expressed in this work are solely those of the author and do not necessarily reflect the views of the publisher. It hereby disclaims any responsibility for them.

Published by Pen Culture Solutions   03/16/2023

Pen Culture Solutions
1-888-727-7204 (USA)
1-800-950-458 (Australia)
support@penculturesolutions.com

Contents

DEDICATION i
PREFACE ii
The Gift of Life 1
Life in the Military 7
High School Education 15
Discovering God's Purpose for my Life. 19
University Education in the USA 25
Pastoral Work in Ghana: 33
Seminary Education in the USA 45
Summary of Pastoral Work in the USA 51
How to be Born Again 57
How to Receive the Baptism of the Holy Spirit 63
How to be Led by the Holy Spirit 67
Biblical People Led by the Holy Spirit 73
The Holy Spirit in the Old Testament 79
Scripture Verses on Being Led by the Holy Spirit 85
The Mark of a Spirit-filled Christian 89
How to Overcome Temptations 95
How to Grow in Christian Maturity 101
How to Please God in Your Life 107
How-to Trust God at All Times 113
The Epilogue 119

DEDICATION

"The Guidance of the Holy Spirit" is dedicated to my lovely and esteemed grandchildren– Jophiel Yenn-Batah and Selasi Yenn-Batah- in hope that as they grow up, they will walk in the Spirit and thus fulfill God's purpose for their lives. Grace, peace, love and God's blessings
be upon you Jophiel and Selasi.
JYB.

PREFACE

We are blessed by the presence of the Holy Spirit in our lives. However, there are too many distractions in this world that lure us away from the presence of God. Yet in the midst of these distractions, noises, temptations, and falling away from the presence of God, we find grace and mercy in the work of Jesus Christ on the Cross at Calvary.

Such grace and mercy found me when I was born. Growing up, I was distracted by the things of this world. Yet, God in his mercy and grace, called me out of my sinful ways, saved me by grace through faith in Jesus Christ and chose me to be his servant in ministry.

" The Guidance of the Holy Spirit" is about how I became a Christian, being called into ministry, being led by the Holy Spirit in my life and Pastoral Ministry over fifty years.

Sharing my story, I hope, will inspire readers to draw closer to God in their lives and to experience the joy of the presence of the Holy Spirit. This new experience starts with being Born Again.

Not only do I share my testimony but also I give guidance on how to be saved by the grace of God through faith in Jesus Christ, how to be Baptized with the Holy Spirit to give you power to live for God and how to live a life pleasing to God.

My sincere thanks and gratitude go to all the people God put in my life to help me fulfill God's purposes for my life— my family, friends, relatives, classmates, Pastors and Bishops that I served under in Africa, Europe and the United States of America.

Also, thank you to Rev Kate Thompson and Rev. Eno Afon, my Associate Pastors at Wesley United Methodist Church in Arlington Texas for their dedication

and service to the Lord.

Glory be to God Almighty the Father, Son and the Holy Spirit for grace, mercy, love, guidance and provision for my life. I am eternally grateful to God for calling me out of the Army to serve Him as Fisher of men and women perishing in sin in this world. Indeed, God took away my Army gun and gave me the Bible as my new weapon to save souls.. It is a great honor to be a Soldier in the Army of the Lord!

Praise be unto God Almighty for ever and ever. Amen.

CHAPTER 1

The Gift of Life

Greetings in the name of the Father, Son and the Holy Spirit. In this book, I testify about the work of the Holy Spirit in my life in order to encourage people to surrender their lives to God and to receive the Holy Spirit to guide them in their lives.

You may be wondering what is the Holy Spirit? Well, the Holy Spirit is the Lord and Giver of life. He is Creator Spirit, present before the creation of the universe and through his power everything was made in Jesus Christ by God the Father.

The work of the Holy Spirit is to exalt Christ in our hearts. He forms the image of Christ in us and we owe all to God in salvation. The Father gave us His Son, the Son gave his life for us, and the Holy Spirit gives us life and faith in Christ. This is the Spirit that has been in my life and has helped me to serve the Lord faithfully in ministry for many decades. The Holy Spirit is a gift we receive when we are born again by accepting Jesus Christ as our Lord and Savior and are baptized in his in the name of the Father, Son and the Holy Spirit.

Hello, my name is Jackson Yenn-Batah, a trained Theologian and Pastor. I was born in a village called Bano-Kpezie in the Upper West Region of Ghana near Nadowli, the District Capital. My parents were uneducated farmers who lived in Bano (Riverside) without electricity and pipe water then. My father was Issaka Kpemuo and my mother was Dankyima Kpemuo. I am the fourth born in the family of six. I had two senior brothers and a sister before me and two brothers after me. I was born in the late 1940s.

When I was just three years old, I was taken to the Southern part of Ghana then known as the Gold Coast Colony under the British Empire. My Uncle who was called Mahama, had left home early in his twenties to join the Gold Coast Police Force. After being away for almost five years, he visited home on leave one day and when he was returning to his station, he took me with him to live with him. Years later he explained to me why he took me with him.

In our culture, which is the Dagaaba culture, two brothers can exchange their sons with each other to cement their family ties. That is exactly what happened in my case. So technically I became the son of my Uncle and couldn't call him Uncle anymore but my Father. I believe God was working in my situation to glorify his name by sending me to the Southern part of Ghana to get the opportunity to have education in order to serve him. The Northern Territories where I was born was not as developed as the Gold Coast Colony –the Southern part of the country now called Ghana after independence in 1957. The Southern part of Ghana had more schools and this afforded me the opportunity to be educated.

When I left home, I was almost three years old. In those colonial days, there were few pre-K schools to attend and they were very expensive. Those of us who did not come from rich families, had to grow to be six before going to government public school. Therefore, in my case, I had to spend time growing up in the Police Barracks before starting first grade.

At the time I started school, we were stationed in a town called Kibi in Akyem Abuakwa in the Eastern Region of Ghana. I spent three years attending first to third grade. Then we were transferred to Koforidua in the Eastern Region of Ghana where I continued my education from the fourth to fifth grade. While completing the fifth grade, we were transferred to Cape Coast in the Central Region of Ghana- a coastal city known for its first class educational institutions. There I continued from the fifth to sixth

grades before attending one of the best Middle Schools - the Cape Coast

Methodist Middle School at Baka Akyir near St Augustine College.

My first experience of becoming a Christian was when I was attending the Koforidua Anglican Primary School in the fourth grade. This was a mission school. We were required to attend Church Service on Sundays and morning worship at an assembly before school starts every morning. Through this process, the Chaplain of the school made sure that we were baptized even though many of us didn't know what baptism meant.

I was one of the pulpils baptized when I was in the 5th grade. My given Christian name is Jackson- a derivative of John in the Gospels. My surname which is Yenn-Batah is my birth name. In our culture, when a baby is born , the Elders of the village in consultation with the family of the baby, gather on the seventh day to name the baby in a special ceremony early in the morning. Names have meanings in our culture. Yenn-Batah means either lack of wisdom or gifted with wisdom. The word "yenn" in my language means wisdom. The word "batah" means either "lack of" or "triple". The Elders choose to name me "yenn- batah" with the positive interpretation of "gifted with wisdom". Not long after my baptism at the Koforidua Anglican Primary School, we were transferred to Cape Coast where I completed my Primary School education and continued at Methodist Middle School. The Methodist Church that administered the Middle School, got us involved in Christian Education both in school and at Church. It was compulsory for all students attending Methodist Schools to attend Methodist Church in the town on Sundays to worship and names of attendees were recorded for Monday roll call at School. All those who did not attend Church Service on Sundays were punished at school. So I grew up attending the Methodist Church by force and through this, I learned to sing many hymns from the Methodist hymn book. Infact, I had a pocket sized Methodist hymn book that I always carried in my back pocket wherever I went.

While in Middle School, I performed very well academically and sat for the Common Entrance examination when I was in Form 2 in order to attend High School. In those days, bright students who passed the Common Entrance conducted by the West African Examination Council could go to High School before completing Form 4 which is the last grade in Middle School.

Fortunately, I passed both the Common Entrance and the interview to attend Mfantsipim Secondary School in Cape Coast but could not afford to attend High School because of lack of financial support. As a result, I had to continue my education in Middle School and completed Middle School Form 4.

In my final year in Middle School, my father Mahama who was then stationed in a town called Apam in the Central Region of Ghana, felt suddenly sick after eating in a chop-bar (restaurant) while on duty in another village. He was taken to the Winneba Hospital where he had surgery and died a few days later. His autopsy confirmed that he died of food poisoning. With his passing away, I was left on my own without any financial support. Therefore, I had to wash and iron Police uniforms for the Police men in Barrack to earn income to take care of my needs till I graduated from the Middle School at the age of fifteen.

CHAPTER 2

Life in the Military

While thinking about what to do after graduating from Middle School, there were two options left for me. The first was to attend Pulpils Teachers' Training School in order to become a pupil teacher after School. There were many Teachers' Training Schools sponsored by the Government provided one passed the Entrance examination and allowances were paid to students. I felt that this was the best option for me if I wanted to advance in life with a professional job.

However, while I was thinking about this option seriously, a man from the Army visited the Police Barracks where I was living. He came to visit his brother who was a police officer. Many of us– the boys in Barracks, were very impressed by the neatness of his uniform and how sharp he looked. We had conversations with him about what life was in the Army. We heard many impressive stories, education in the Army, and opportunity for advancement in the Army through promotions. Many of us were impressed and interested so we found out when recruitment will take place. Armed with this information, I decided to join the Army instead of attending Pulpil Training School to become a teacher.

Early the following year after graduation in the Fall, I went to the Recruiting Center in Kumasi in the Ashanti Region of Ghana to join the Army. I was fifteen years old and one of the Officers recruiting us told me I was too young to join the Army and advised me to go home and grow up before coming to join the Army but I persisted. I told him I wanted to join and grow in the Army. He couldn't convince me to drop out of recruitment and so I was recruited for basic training in March 1963.

My Platoon number was 89 and my enlisted number was 161928. Our Basic training was for three months. In the basic training, we learned shooting, drill, swimming, physical education, endurance training, and other trainings necessary to become a good soldier. My Platoon was one of many platoons that were under basic training in the Army then. Any platoon that passed out was transferred to join any of the regular Army units in the various battalions in the country.

After my basic training, I and other members of my platoon were specifically selected and posted to the President's Own Guard Regiment in Accra the Capital City of Ghana to be part of the elite soldiers who guarded the President of the Republic of Ghana. Those of us who were transferred to this Regiment, were given additional special training in advance weaponry, tactical defense and security details in order to be ready to protect the President of the Republic.I spent two years guarding the President at his residence and office. I also traveled with my colleagues as advance party to anywhere the President was to visit to secure the place for his safety before his arrival. After my second year in the Army, I had the opportunity to switch from guard duties to the Signal branch of my battalion to train as Signal man–communication man. In the Signal branch, I was trained in various aspects of communications especially by learning Morse Code as a way of military communication. In those days, there were no cellphones, internet, and other means of modern communications. All communications were done mostly by voice, by way of telephone and by telegraph. To communicate in telegraph, one had to learn the Morse code. My training lasted twelve weeks at the Signal Headquarters in Burma Camp and I passed my training and returned to my regiment to serve in the Signal branch.

Back to my Regiment, I was promoted to the rank of Lance Corporal and assigned to all communications involving top priority cases. Because of the training I had was based on British Military equipments, I was also trained in how to use Russian Commutations equipment in order to perform my duties well. I had Russian instructors and interpreters train me for the job. After all these trainings, I served as one of the youngest and the best Military communicators in my battalion assigned to top priority and sensitive military communications. It was in this position that I served until the President of Ghana was overthrown in a bloody coup d'etat in 1966.

It was on Monday January 24, 1966 early in the morning that the coup d'etat was completed. The Sunday night prior to early Monday, my regiment was summoned by an alarm. This meant that every member of the Regiment was to dress in warfare uniform and assembly at the parade ground. Within a short period according to our training, everyone was at the assembly ground ready for instructions from the various unit commanders.

Convoys of military trucks, armor cars and other necessary equipments were put in place. We were instructed by our Commanding Officers to join the trucks by Platoon. We did and in a few minutes we were on our way to a location we were not told except the drivers and the Commanders.

Since it was night, it was difficult for me to see where the trucks were heading. In about twenty minutes later, we landed at the Flagstaff House where the President lived. Already, there was shooting going on and artilleries shelling bombs into the President's resident and the compound. We took positions to do battle with the enemy forces. Since we were from the President's Own Guard Regiment, our duty was to protect the President and his family.

We did battle with the enemy forces to save the Presidency and the Republic of Ghana but we were defeated after more than three hours exchange of fire.

There were two major reasons we were defeated: the President had traveled out of the country on a peace mission and as a result, we had a stand-down by withdrawing our artilleries and tanks to another distant location and by the time message went for reinforcement, it was too late because the enemy forces had come prepared with all their fire power against us. The second reason is that we run out of ammunition because we were not given enough supply of ammunition. Apparently, the Commander did not anticipate that this was a coup d'etat and did not prepare us for it.

As a signal man, it was my first experience in battle. I was receiving messages from other Commanders for my Commander while being shelled with bullets over my head in my bunker. There were granates thrown at me, but they landed far away from me. It was bloody coup d'etat. Many soldiers and innocent civilians were killed. Many early passengers traveling in buses and cars to work were caught in crossfire and died tragically on the road between Flagstaff House and 37 Military Hospital.

These were workers at the Airport.

When the battle was over, I found some of my Platoon mates death.

Those of us alive, were asked to go back to Barracks. The coup d'etat had succeeded and the enemy forces that were part of the Ghana Armed Forces did not think it was necessary to pursue us because we were part of the Ghana Armed Forces. Their main objective was to everthrow the President and since that was achieved, there was no need to cause harm to us.

Back in the Barracks, we learned more about the coup d'etat and the people involved. A new military government was formed with the coup leaders forming a Military Council to rule the Republic of Ghana. The President's Own Guard Regiment was disbanded and those of us in that Regiment, were posted to other Battalions in Ghana. I was posted together with some other soldiers in my unit to the Second Battalion of Infantry at Apremudo in Takoradi in the Western Region of Ghana. It took us about three weeks after the coup d'etat to finally leave Burma Camp our station to the new Battalion in Takoradi.

My life in the new Battalion was smooth but boring to me. I did not have the joy that I had before the Coup d'etat anymore. At my age of almost eighteen, I started reflecting on life and the purpose of life. If I had died at this young age, what would have been my achievement on earth I thought.

For the first time in my life since I joined the Army, I started taking my Christian life seriously. I had not been to Church since I joined the Army and had stopped praying or reading the Bible. Now, I started reading some Christian tracks distributed by some street Evangelists but would not go to Church on Sundays to worship. About six months later, at my new station, the Holy Spirit started ministering to my soul and I started praying and reading the Bible.

One day, I heard the Holy Spirit speak to me. " Jackson, I have work for you to do but you cannot do it unless you attend High School". When I heard this, I believed that God was speaking to me by the Spirit.

I argued with the Lord about this and gave all kinds of excuses as to why I didn't think it was a good idea to leave the Army and go to study in Highschool. Who will pay my School fees and where will I get money to take care of myself? These were paramount questions I asked the Lord but I didn't get any answers. I decided that I wasn't going to leave the Army where I had income security to go walking in a wilderness and suffer of hunger, thirst and want. So I didn't take the message seriously. This happened around March when I turned 18.

For the next three months, the Spirit kept nagging me with the the same message but I refused to listened or to accept the offer to leave the Army and go get more education in Highschool for a job I didn't know.

Then one day, the Holy Spirit made his last move. He referred me to the life of Moses in the Bible and to Hebrew 11: 24-26.

" By faith Moses when he was grown up, refused to be called the son of Pharaoh's daughter, choosing rather to share ill- treatment with the people of God than to enjoy the fleeting pleasures of sin. He considered abuse suffered for the Christ greater wealth than the treasures of Egypt, for he looked to the reward".

This passage challenged me about my faith and obedience to Christ. I felt the Lord was calling me into something very challenging and fruitful but I didn't know what it was. He needed me to take a leap of faith into the future.

Well, for several months, I was faced with this call to leave the Army and go to High School. I remembered the story of Abraham, how God called him to leave his family and people to go to the land that God will show him. I remembered how Abraham by faith left Ur, his hometown,and everything and followed God's command. (Genesis 12:1). Eventually, I gave in to the call and by faith began searching for a school to attend. The government and public schools were out of the question because one could only attend at a particular age and pass an entrance examination. I couldn't be admitted into such schools at age 18 when many high school students were graduating from High School.Therefore, I started searching for a good private high school where age was not a factor in admittance and found one called the Royal Academy in a town called Winneba in the Central Region of Ghana.

The fees for attending Royal Academy was very high but I was able to pay a year's school fees before leaving the Army to start my High School education in the Spring of 1967.

Having paid my school fee for one academic year, It was time to get out of the Army to go to school. Because I had served in the Army less than the six years required to be discharged, I had to apply for discharge with good reason. I made an appointment to see my Commanding Officer for discharge and when the day came, I was matched into his Office to answer questions about my request to be discharged. He asked me reasons I wanted to be discharged.

I explained that I was aspiring to become a Commissioned Officer in the

Army in future (though that was not my true intent) and needed to improve upon my education by attending High School I was therefore seeking discharge to attend High School. I showed him the receipt for the school fees I had paid and pleaded to be discharged.

Impressed by my ambition, determination and my explanation, he made the necessary recommendation to the Army Headquarters for me to be discharged from the Army for further studies. I waited for my discharge and in the last week of December 1966, I became a civilian.

CHAPTER 3

High School Education

In the new year of January 1967, I was enrolled at the Royal Academy to begin my studies. I arrived on campus and met the headmaster who interviewed me and decided that because I had studied Mathematics, Physics, English, Geography in the Army, I was to start my studies in Form 2 instead of Form 1 the beginning grade.

My studies in Royal Academy was excellent but also challenging in the areas of French and Latin which were required subjects to study. Because I didn't start from the lowest grade, I missed learning the foundamentals of the Languages involving Lexis and Structure in addition to conjugations of verbs. Nevertheless, I put in extra effort to catch up in French and Latin. Gradually,I started enjoying my studies and made good friends because everyone knew I was from the Army and wanted to be nice to me before they got into trouble with me. I spent one and half years at the Royal Academy studying English Language, French, Latin, English Literature, Geography, History, Bible Knowledge, Mathematics, Physics, Chemistry and Biology.

By the Fall of the 1968/69 Academic year, I was in Form 4. Before this time,

things were not going well in the School. The Founder decided to relocate the School to another town for financial reasons.

Royal Academy was a private High School in a private rented property without funding from the government. It depended on high enrollment to make payroll and to meet the administrative needs of the school. Enrollment was dwindling and rate of rented property was high. It seems the Landlord wanted to raise the rent which the Founder was not prepared to pay. Secondly, because of financial difficulties in securing more funds to run the school, teachers were leaving because of lack of salary payment. In addition, feeding of boarding house students became a big problem. Food for students during dinning time became irregular and poor. Hence the desire to relocate. Many of the students did not like the idea because we were going to loose many of the good tutors we had. Many of the subject Masters we had were highly trained in the Universities and employed at the Winneba Teachers' Training College. They were part- time teachers in the Royal Academy. and there was no way they were going to move if the school relocated to another town far away.. In view this, many of the students decided to transfer to other schools. In my case, I left Winneba to Accra the Capital City of Ghana to search for a good school to continue my education. I first tried many Schools in Accra but could not get admission because the classes were full and there were students on waiting list. In the end, the Holy Spirit led me to a mission school called Saint Stephen's Secondary School.

This was a mission school operated under the auspices of the Christian Methodist Episcopal Church of the United States of America and had some good teachers. I was admitted into Form 4 in the Fall of 68/69 Academic Year. I spent the 1968/69 and the 1969/70 at St. Stephen's Secondary School and graduated in May 1970 from High School and was immediately employed in September 1970 when our results were out from the West Africa Examination Council and I had passed all my subjects. I was appointed to be the House Master of the Boys' Dormitory and to teach English Language.

For the next two years, I taught in the School and served in the Christian Methodist Episcopal Church in Accra as an Evangelist.

In the Spring of 1972 at the Church's Annual Conference, I was ordained a Deacon in the Church by Bishop Randolph Peter Shy of the United States of America who was in charge of the Ghana, Nigeria and the Liberia Annual Conferences. Thereafter, I enrolled in the Gospel International Riverside School of Preaching in Nerebehi near Kumasi to train for Pastoral Work in the Church.

It was during this time that I had a total transformation of my life through the power of the Holy Spirit.

CHAPTER 4

Discovering Gods' Purpose for my Life.

Even though I served as Evangelist for the Church, I didn't have the perception that it was God leading me in that direction until I entered Bible College. At the Gospel International Riverside School of Preaching, I learned a lot about the work of God and about the Holy Spirit's work in my life.

We had rigid schedule for Studies, Prayers, Preaching and Evangelism. The most fascinating one for me was prayers. Even though we had our individual prayer times, it was mandatory for all of us to gather at 3:00pm every afternoon to pray together. This was not like the usual way of praying by reciting some written or memorized prayers. This was power-packed extempore prayers uttered by individuals in the prayer group as led by the Holy Spirit.

It was during one of these afternoon prayer meetings that the Lord spoke to us about His purpose for bringing us together at the Bible College. The message came to us in a prophecy by one of us. While we were praying together, the Holy Spirit overshadowed one us and the person started prophecing: " My children, I have brought you here to reveal my purpose for your lives. I want you to carry the message of Salvation to the world and my Spirit will be with you always". That was my first time of hearing and seeing someone speak in tongues and giving a prophecy. The prayer room was filled with the presence of the Holy Spirit and we were in awe and trembling at the power and presence of the Holy Spirit. Many of my mates started crying and confessing their sins. In my case, I was trembling with fear and repeating the sentence:"Lord I believe. Lord have mercy upon me". It was like I was in the presence of God and being judged of my sins. I couldn't stand in the presence of this powerful God and the presence of the Holy Spirit so I had to fall upon my knees and eventually prostrate in the presence of

God and submit my life to him. That was my first encounter with the presence of the Holy Spirit in my life.

At another time, we were at prayer meeting at the same room. Whenever we gathered to pray, it was cooperate prayer time. Usually we had a leader who led us through various prayer topics. This time as we were praying, some school children passing by after school, came to stand at one of the windows to watch us pray. While we were praying the Holy Spirit baptized one of the school girls of about twelve years old and lead her into the prayer room. As soon she entered, she fell on the floor, started crying and rolling on floor. All of a sudden, the Holy Spirit started speaking to us through the girl about the Lord Jesus Christ. The prophecy came from Isaiah Chapter 9:2-7. "The people who walked in darkness have seen a great light; those who dwell in the land of deep darkness, on them have light shined----".

Before this, the Holy Spirit commanded us to open to the Book of Isaiah chapter 9. By the time I opened my Bible, this girl filled with the Holy Spirit was reciting this chapter word by word in English and another tongue that I did not understand. As much as I tried to read along, she was so fast that I could not catch up with her prophecing. Listening to the prophecy coming through this girl, made me believe in the Living God. In deed God is a Living God and his Spirit works in peoples lives to bring transformation. That day, I affirmed my faith in God and my commitment to serve him all the days of my life seeing and experiencing his work in our midst.

My third experience with the Holy Spirit was at another prayer meeting. This time it was a night prayer meeting in a classroom.

That prayer session started at 10:00 pm at night on Friday night to midnight. We had prayed continuously for two hours and brought the session to a close a little after midnight. I remember every one leaving but I was still stuck in my seat. I couldn't move even though I wanted to. All of a sudden I felt the Holy Spirit working in my life. First I was filled with the Spirit. Then I started shaking and sweating. The next thing I experienced was like a child born anew and being washed in water. That experience lasted for about thirty minutes and gradually I came to myself. The Holy Spirit had washed me from my sins and I had a new experience of forgiveness of sin and sanctification. It took me some time to leave the prayer room and when I left I remembered the passage in 2 Corinthians 5:17 " Therefore if anyone is in Christ, he is a new creature, the old things have passed away, behold new things have come". Indeed that night, I became born again and even though many years ago I had baptism by sprinkling, I went for baptism by immersion in the Nerebehi River close to the School a few days later.

After this experience, I continued with my studies till my final year when something miraculously happened to me. We were on Summer break and I decided to visit my cousin in Accra the capital city of Ghana.

No sooner had I arrived than I felt seriously sick.

My body temperature was high and I felt burning sensation all over my body. I couldn't take a bath for almost a month. Anytime water touched my body it was like pouring water on a hot iron. I went to the hospital but they could not find what was wrong with me. It seems my sickness was spiritual. It was Satan attacking me.

For nearly a month, I was restricted to my bed praying for healing and reading the Bible. My cousin got very concerned and invited other family members from other towns to come check my situation. When they finally came to see me, they concluded that I was sick to the point of death and the option for them was to transport me home. When they consulted me, I refused to be sent home because I believed I was going to get well. Disappointed by my decision, they left for their various destinations. This happened in the third week of my sickness. Then something miraculously happened in the fourth week of my sickness.

I had a dream. In the dream, Jesus and his disciples were sitting under a big tree planted in an ocean. I could see the roots of the tree in the water. Jesus was standing on the biggest root and his disciples on much smaller roots. I was standing on a root hair which was much smaller than all the roots. I looked at Jesus' face from where I was standing. Jesus said to me "Fall into the river". I responded "If I fall into the water, I will die". Jesus then asked me to look at my left. Looking, I saw women at a well struggling to fetch water. They were fighting over the water in the bucket that was used to fetch the water from the well. The problem was that each was impatient to wait for her turn. So when the water in the bucket came up, each struggled to get it first. In doing so they lost the water in the bucket. Jesus instructed me go help them. I did. I fetched the water for them one by one till they all left with water. After that I reported back to Jesus. He showed me a bright city very far away and instructed me to go serve him there.

Then I woke up from my dream and realized that I have been miraculously healed.. All my pains were gone and my body was not tormenting me any more. I jumped out from the bed and for the first time in many days, I was able to have a shower. A few days later, I was back to seminary to complete my studies. That experience affirmed that it was this work that the Lord spoke to me about when I was in the Army. That was when I discovered God's purpose for my life and my commission to serve the Lord Jesus Christ in the dream.

CHAPTER 5

University Education in the USA

After my training at the Riverside School of Preaching, I was sent to Odumase, a town near Sunyani to establish a High School for the Gospel International Incorporated. It was the Spring of 1973. when I arrived in the town and met the two Chiefs in the town, the Elders, and Community Leaders to announce to them my purpose for the town under the auspicies of the Gospel International Incorporated. I was warmly welcome and I formed a Committee with the Elders to implement my plan for a High School to be established and opened in the Fall of 1973.

By early September, I had succeeded in securing a place to start the High School. Classrooms were ready, Boarding houses for boys and girls were also in place. The last thing I did was to interview and hire teachers for the School. By the third week of September, the Gospel International Secondary School was ready to open at Odumase near Sunyani in the Brong Ahafo Region of Ghana to the glory and honor of the Lord. Years later, the school was taken over by the people of Odumase and the Government and renamed the school Odumaseman Secondary School. Today, it has educated thousands of students from the whole of the Brong Ahafo Region and many parts of Ghana.

In the last week of September, I left Odumase to Accra, the capital city of

Ghana to serve my Denomination as an Evangelist. From the Fall of 1973 to the Spring of 1976, I served in this position without any stipend.. To support myself and the ministry that I love, I gained employment at the Ghana Medical School of the University of Ghana as Library Assistant at the Korle Bu Teaching Hospital from 1974 to 1977 when I was employed as the Librarian of Aquinas Secondary School at Osu. While working as Librarian,

I studied for the Advanced Level Certificate and passed the West African Examination Council "A" Level examination in 1978 and applied for further studies in the USA. My admission was accepted by Texas College in Tyler Texas in 1979. Texas College was one of the Colleges established by my denomination in the USA to educate students.

I left Ghana in January 1980 to pursue further studies in the United States of America.

Before then, during the Ghana Annual Conference of the Christian Methodist Episcopal Church in Ghana in February 1976, I was ordained an Elder of the CME Church by Bishop Madison Exum who was then in charge of the Ghana Annual Conference of the CME Church and appointed the Chaplain of Christian Methodist Secondary School in Accra where I served till January 1980 when I left Ghana for further studies in the United States of America: first, at Texas College in Tyler, then to the University of Texas at Tyler where I doubled majored in Business Administration with a major in Finance and Political Science.

In May 1983, I graduated with Bachelor degrees in Business Administration and Political Science.

That same year, I enrolled for the Master of Science degree in Public Administration which I completed in the fall of 1984.

Life in America was very interesting and challenging. I first lived in Texas College's Male Housing facility for six months and then moved out to stay in a rented four- bedroom house on West Lawrence Street in Tyler. I had other students from Nigeria who lived in the house with me. We all had a room each and shared the kitchen and living room. I stayed there from Fall 1980 to the Spring of 1986 when I left for Ghana.

Since I didn't have Scholarship for my studies in the USA, I worked myself through College. First, I worked as Kitchen Assistant at Red Barn Steak House in South Broadway Avenue in Tyler from the Fall of 1980 to 1983 when I graduated with my doubled Bachelor degrees. Then I was hired as Gas Station Manager where I had better pay from the Spring of 1984 to January 1986 when I left to Ghana my home country.

Before I left the USA, I had met some American friend at the University whose father was interested in International Business especially in export/ import of timber etc. I had a deal with them to return to Ghana to facilitate this idea of import/ export business. That was my main motivation for returning to Ghana. Little did I know that God had other plans for me in Ghana.

I arrived in Ghana in January 1986. It was the month that Bishop Randolph Peter Shy of the Christian Methodist Episcopal Church in charged of the African Annual Conference, arrived in Ghana for the Ghana Annual Conference. Before I left the USA, I talked to him on phone about my going back to Ghana. I remember him inviting me to the Ghana Annual Conference to be held in January in Ghana. As a respect to him, I honored his invitation during one of the Conference days. He was happy to see me at the Conference and introduced me to the Annual Conference delegates and invited guests. He talked highly about my education and academic achievements in the United States of America and asked me to bring greetings to the Conference. I did and soon after, I left the Conference to attend to the affairs of my new business.

Well, while working on my business plans of registering the business in Ghana and making the necessary arrangements for the export of timber to the USA, I chanced to meet the Secretary of the Ghana Annual Conference of the Christian Methodist Episcopal Church. To my surprise, he said the Conference was over a few days ago and that Bishop Randolph Peter Shy had left a message and a certificate for me. He gave me an envelope that contained a Certificate of appointment as the First Mission Supervisor of the Christian Methodist Episcopal Church in Ghana with instructions for reorganizing the Church in Ghana.

Apparently, from the years that I left Ghana to study in the USA, many of the leaders of the Church had also left Ghana for greener pastures in the USA and other African countries because of Economic hardship in Ghana. It was a period of Military Rule in Ghana and there were shortages of food and essential commodities. Worst of all, there was prolonged draught in Ghana that ushered in famine and people were suffering of hunger. It was so severe that Ghanaians named the period "Rawlings Chain" after the leader of the government in power then. The absence of these Church leaders, weaken the work of the CME Church in Ghana and left a vaccume in the leadership of the Church. It was therefore the hope of Bishop Shy that appointing me the Mission Supervisor, will turn things around for better.

Unfortunately, he did not consult with me about his plans for me in Ghana.

So I took the appointment certificate but reject the money he gave me. I didn't want to have anything to do with the Church in Ghana because of my past experience of working for the Church without any stipend.. I wanted to have a new life with my new business. But that was not the direction the Holy Spirit wanted me to persue.

Yet, I was hard-headed and wanted to run a Business instead of serving the Lord as an ordained minister.

Well for six months, I tried to get the Business off ground but couldn't succeed.

Doing business in Ghana was unlike in the USA where everything goes fast and smoothly. In Ghana you have to grease people's palm if you want things to be done quickly. Even after that, there was no guarantee that you would succeed. For six months, I was tossed around in every Government Department that I needed something done for me. I paid some ridiculous fees and charges demanded by government officials. By June that year 1986, my Business hadn't taken off and I had spent so much on unnecessary expenses that I decided to abort my Business plan and seek employment to support myself.

It was during this period that the Holy Spirit reminded me of the assignment that Bishop Randolph Peter Shy had given me.

I thought about it and concluded that the Lord wanted me to serve him in the Church again even though no salary or operational expenses was available. Finally, I obeyed the voice of the Holy Spirit and took my assignment as the Mission Supervisor of the Church in Ghana without pay.

To support myself, I went to the Public Services Commission to put in an applications for employment in the Government sector.

The good thing about the Commission is that it served as employment Center for graduates from abroad. Once you put in your application, copies are sent to every Government Department seeking qualified graduates to hire. Not long after I put in my application,I started receiving interview letters from various Ministries which I attended and passed. Soon, I started receiving employment letters offering me job in Accounting and Finance Departments of Banks, Tax Companies, Internal Revenue etc. Now it was time for me to choose the best offer. While trying to take a decision based on the reporting date for work, I had a letter from the Asempa Publishers of the Christian Council of Ghana offering me the position of Acquisition Editor in the Publishing House. I had earlier applied for that position and had attended an interview which I passed. The Salary was far better than any of the offers I had received from the Government departments. In addition, I was to have a car, an accommodation, and various allowances. Because I was appointed as the Mission Supervisor of the CME Church which is also a member of the Christian Council of Ghana, I thought it was better to take this position rather than work for the Government of Ghana.

Therefore, in August 1986, I started working in the Publishing House as the first Acquisition Editor while serving the CME Church. In the end, everything worked well for me and I abandoned the Business plan with my United States of America partners.

CHAPTER 6

Pastoral Work in Ghana;

1986-1995

My ministry in Ghana covered two areas: the Christian Methodist Episcopal Church and Asempa Publishers of the Christian Council of Ghana. I will cover each area separately.

Concerning the work of the Christian Methodist Episcopal Church in Ghana, it was truly dead when I took over as Mission Supervisor. The only Church built in Accra, Ghana by the Church in the USA was a small Temple at the Christian Methodist Secondary School at Asylum Down near the Kwame Nkrumah Circle. When I served as Chaplain of the School from 1976-1979 before leaving in January 1980 to the USA to study, it was the Headquarters of the Ghana Annual Conference. It was there that all the Annual Conferences were held. Infact, it was there that the first Annual Conference was held when the mission of the CME Church was organized in Ghana in 1958 by Bishop Elijah Murchison, the first Bishop in charge of the African mission.

But in my absence, no Chaplain was appointed to replace me. Therefore, it was shut down entirety and turned into Music classroom for the students of the Christian Methodist Secondary for all the years I was absent from Ghana.

The next CME Church that was partially operative in Accra was in Accra New Town followed by one in Nsawam in the Eastern Region of Ghana. According to the Annual Conference reports received in 1986, there were several branches of the Church in the Eastern Region of Ghana. But when I visited the various towns to check on these Churches, I found none in existence. Apparently, some people took advantage of the fact that the Bishop couldn't travel to these remote places to to check on things so they duped the Church and received funds for their personal use.

Fortunately, my presence on the scene changed everything. No one could come to the Annual Conference to deceive anyone.

As a result, I started with an empty Beaulah Temple CME Church in Accra. The one in New Town had lost the founder and did not have a trained Pastor to continue with the work of the Church. So it was turned into a classroom for the attached School. The Church in Nsawam was also turned into a School for the founder in order to survive in the difficult Economic situation in Ghana.

The challenge then was for me to grow a new congregation at Beaulah Temple and to assist in the growth of the other two branches while aiming to open more branches.

As I was working on my strategic plan to grow the CME Church in Ghana, a General Conference of the Christian Methodist Episcopal Church took place in the USA in May 1986 and Bishop Shy was retired. A New Episcopal District- The Tenth Episcopal District- was created and Bishop Nathaniel Linsey was appointed to supervise the 10th Episcopal District which included Ghana, Nigeria and Liberia.

Bishop Linsey knew me long before he was elected Bishop and we had a very good relationship. He was elected to the Episcopacy in 1978 and visited Ghana in 1979 when he was in charge of the Seventh Episcopal District in the USA. I was the Chaplain of the Christian Methodist Secondary School in Accra and was his host during his visit to Ghana. He and his entourage were very impressed by my work at the School. That was the beginning of our friendship.

So when he was appointed to supervise the work in Ghana, he was happy that I was in Ghana in 1987 to receive him.

When he attended his first Annual Conference in Ghana in 1987, I shared with him the problems facing the Mission work in Ghana and the plan I had to grow the Church in Ghana.

Foremost was the problem of a Court case against the Church in Ghana. Some of the former leaders had used the name of the Church to credit tickets from a traveling agent promising to pay for the tickets after returning from the USA from a Conference but they did not honor their promises because they never returned to Ghana to fulfill their financial obligations to the Travel Agency.

So when I appeared on the scene, I was served with Court papers.

The second problem was that the Church had lost her membership in the Christian Council of Ghana for non- payment of membership dues.

Thirdly, there was no Central Office for the administration of the Church in Ghana. In effect, nothing was going on for the Mission in Ghana. It was therefore

a heavy burden laid on me to grow the Church under such circumstances but I took the challenge and with the support of Bishop Linsey, I was able to turn things around by the time I was ready to leave Ghana to the USA for further Theological Studies. I must stress that during my nine years work for Christian Methodist Episcopal Church in Ghana from 1986-1995, I was not paid any monthly salary. The meager money given annually at the Annual Conferences, was used to train new leaders, pay new pastors' stipend, and for administrative work for the Church. My salary and allowances from Asempa Publishers was what sustained me and my family all these years. Infact, I invested much of my salary from Asempa Publishers into the Mission work in Ghana to ensure that the Church survived.

Well, how did I turn things around for the Church?

I won the case against the Church in Court and saved the property of the Church that they were going after. I also used my position at the Christian Council of Ghana to restore the Church's membership. Lastly, I renovated Beulah Temple, opened a Bank Account, organized crusades that helped me grow the Church with new members. By the third year of my work in the Church, I had succeeded in bringing the CME Church in Ghana back to life. When Bishop Shy accompanied Bishop Linsey to the Ghana Annual Conference in 1988, he was very

happy to see the total transformation of the Church. At that Annual Conference, he preached his last sermon in Ghana based on the Book of Esther. His text was from Esther 4:14 and the topic was " You were born for such a time like this".

As I listened to his sermon, I realized and understood why he appointed me three years earlier to head the Church in Ghana.

He realized that with my educational background and experience in ministry, I was the only hope for the Church in Ghana. Therefore, my appointment was critical to the growth of the Church in Ghana. Now he could see the fruit of my labor and rejoiced that I had fufilled his vision for the Church in Ghana.

Unfortunately, that was his last visit to Ghana. The next time I met him was in Arlington Texas at the 1990 General Conference. Two years later, he passed in Atlanta Georgia. I wasn't in the United States of America for his funeral but when I returned to the USA in 1995, I visited his graveside at Lincoln Memorial Gardens to pay my last respect. He passed at 92 years old.

Meanwhile, I continued to grow the Church in Ghana by opening a second branch in Accra New Town (Bishop Linsey CME Church), one at Tesano in Accra (Bethel CME Church), one in Nsawam in the Eastern Region (Nsawam CME Church), another at Pig Farm in Accra (Pig Farm CME Church), and another at Bortianor in the Greater Accra Region.

I also brought in two young men from our Church in Nigeria to help nurture these new Churches. In the year 1994, Bishop Linsey was reassigned to the 2nd Episcopal District in the USA and a new Bishop was assigned to Ghana, Nigeria and Liberia.

His name was Bishop Charles Helton. He was elected at the 1994 General Conference. I had my last Annual Conference with him in Ghana in January 1995 and had the opportunity to withnes the ordination of four new Deacons for the new Churches organized under my supervision. One of them, years later, was elected the first Ghanaian CME Bishop. . In the same year,1995, my second son Andrew was born on Sunday April 16, 1995 on Easter Sunday morning and I left Ghana in August that year to the USA for further Theological studies at the Interdenominational Theological Center in Atlanta Georgia.

My assignment to grow the CME Church in Ghana was done and the Christian Methodist Episcopal Church in Ghana was revived and growing strong. It wasn't easy reviving the CME Church in Ghana when funds were not given to grow the Church. Even with sacrifices from my personal financial resources, I had members who assumed that because I was the Mission Supervisor, I was given a lot of money by the Church in the USA. But that wasn't so.

I think Church Denominations like the CME Church should not practise Colonialism in Africa. They wait for local people to start Churches and they come in to take over for administrative purposes and not invest a dime into the work of the Lord in Africa. Today, it is happening in Africa. They take over, elect foreign bishops to be in charge of the African Conferences and they are proud of that. Even for an African to be elected a Bishop of the Denomination, they elect the African on a separate ballot and not on the regular ballot as token Bishop. If they don't want African Bishops to oversee any Annual Conference in the USA ,why should the Denomination elect American Bishops to oversee the Annual Conferences in Africa? That is colonialism and racism. The Church must come clean on this issue in Africa now. I pray that African Christian leaders will not allow themselves to be marginalized from their main stream denominations through neo- colonialism and racism by the Church in America. Africans should not allow any American denomination to use African Churches to facilitate their tourism interests instead of doing serious mission work in the context of the Great Commission. When I was Mission Supervisor, much of the budget allocated for the African work, was spent on travels, hotel accommodations, excetra and nothing was left for meaningful mission work. That is not the way to do effective Mission work. That must change.

My other assignment as the Acquisition Editor of Asempa Publishers also had challenges. There were few published books to market to truly make the Publishing House financially strong. We needed to produce more new and exciting titles for the market. The motto of the Publishing House is "Producing Books for Church and State" so I decided to produce new tittles to cover these areas for the market. With a degree in Finance and Marketing from the University of Texas at Tyler in the USA, I decided to conduct a market survey to identify books that were needed for Church and State. The results were eye opening. Books were needed for Christian Education in Churches, Books for Junior and High School in the areas of English Language, Mathematics, Religious Study, and Books for Political Education in Ghana.

Based on this, I had to identify authors that I could work with to produce manuscripts for these subject areas. So I went to the University of Ghana in Accra, Ghana to talk to Professors in the Departments of Political Science, Institute of African Studies, Business Administration, the Department for Religion, and Professors at the leading Seminary in Ghana called Trinity Theological Seminary to share my objectives with them and to commission them to produce various manuscripts for me.

I also went to the Ministry of Education to talk to some seasoned Educationists to produce important books for Primary, Middle and High School students

Above all, I went to Trinity Theological Seminary at Legon to engage the Theologians and to encourage them to produce religious books for the Church in Ghana.

Many of the people I contacted, were very interested in joining in my manuscript production project. Therefore, to engage them, I gave each one of them an assignment. The assignment was to identify a topic in their area of expertise that will address important issues in the Churches, the Schools, and the State. They were to write a synopsis about the subject for me to see and approve for development.

My aim was to see these synopsis first and to determine whether they were what I needed or not, correct or suggest ways to develop the synopsis before any Publisher/Author Contract was signed.

In the first year of my appointment, I persued this approach to the end of the year and in the second year, I signed Publishers/Author contract with most of them to produce manuscripts for publishing with Asempa Publishers of the Christian Council of Ghana. These manuscripts covered the areas that I discovered in my survey.

I was constantly in touch with each author as each developed their manuscript, chapter by chapter to ensure quality write ups and to meet deadlines for production.

By the middle of the second year, some of these manuscripts were completely devoped and submitted to me to edit and pass on to the Production Department for final editing and production. New published titles were getting ready for the Christmas book market while other manuscripts were in the pipeline for publishing.

In the third year of my appointment at Asempa Publishers, we started seeing an increase in Book sales because of the new titles. There were new supplementary reading books for Schools in Ghana, Books for Churches in theology, devotions Christian Education, books on Politics in the areas of Church and State, books on Social Studies et cetera. By this time, I had increased total titles on our published catalog by almost fifty percent. But there were more new titles to come out of production in the following year 1990.

In 1989, our Marketing Manager resigned to take a new Marketing Manager position at one our major book buyers: Challenge Bookshop and we hired a new Marketing Manager to push sales for us. We had all these new and old titles to promote and needed a good Marketing Manager to do that for us. In 1990, more new titles were coming out of the Production Department for sale. We were now at peak production and sale of books. Reprints were being done to meet demands and our cash flow situation had improved dramatically. That summer I took leave to travel to Arlington Texas in the USA in July to attend the General Conference of my denomination the Christian Methodist Episcopal Church and to visit friends in Tyler, Texas and my Alma Mater the University of Texas at Tyler. I spent a month and returned in late July. That was the year my first son Samuel was born in my absence on July 6, 1990.

Back to Ghana in late July, I went back to work and it didn't take long when the new Marketing Manager also resigned to travel to the USA for further studies. In his absence, instead of hiring a new Marketing Manager, the Board of Trustees of Asempa Publishers decided to move me to head the Marketing Department as Marketing Manager of Asempa Publishers in view of the fact that I had a degree in Business Administration with a major in Finance and Marketing. I took the new position and the irony was for me to promote the published new titles I had developed in the Acquisition Department.

To do that, I started traveling extensively to meet Bookshop Managers all over the country to promote sales and to discover new sales outlets for our products. I went from Region to Region and was very successful in making good contacts with Bookshop Manager, individual Book sales agents, Head Masters of Secondary Schools to promote hymn books and other relevant supplementary reading books in Middle Schools. Once this was done, our sales increased because we had more outlets that carried our titles. I also introduced a system of supplying books to these outlets on invoices for sale and for payment quarterly. This means they order titles and quantity needed, I supply them for sale and receive payments monthly or every quarter. This plan worked very well to our mutual interest.

From the time I became Marketing Manager, I started traveling to Germany to participate in the Annual Book Fair held in Frankfurt, Germany to promote our titles under the sponsorship of the World Council Churches. That experience also gave us the opportunity to meet representatives of Christian publishing Companies from Africa, India, Europe, the USA, the Philippines and other countries to make friends, learn new Publishing trends, and make deals on copyright sales.

Out of these contacts, I had invitions to travel to Nairobi, Kenya and Dodoma, Tanzania to train Marketing Managers for Publishing Houses in those countries.

Combining two jobs at the same time, I also traveled to Kenya, Nigeria, Tanzania and back to Germany for short mission work with the Anglican Church, the Christian Methodist Episcopal Church and the World Council of Churches.

By 1994, I was back to the USA for the General Conference of the Christian Methodist Episcopal Church held in Memphis Tennessee. It was at this Conference that I met the Dean of Phillips School of Theology, the Seminary for the CME Church and made arrangements to attend Seminary the following year1995 to study for the Master of Divinity degree at the Interdenominational Theological Center in Atlanta Georgia where Phillips School of Theology is part of the Theological Center.

Upon my return to Ghana, I started preparing for my studies and in the following year, I left Ghana to study and to settle in America. Both my work at the Church and at Asempa Publishers were very fruitful to the glory and honor of the Lord because in all my work, I was led and empowered by the Holy Spirit. In sum, I spent nine years in Ghana before finally moving back in 1995 to study and naturalize in the United States of America.

CHAPTER 7

Seminary Education in the USA

1995-2001

While serving the Church in Ghana, I felt that I needed more Theological education in order to be more effective in ministry. During all this time that I served as the Mission Supervisor and Pastor, I had only graduated from a two-year Bible College with only a Diploma in Theology. My degrees in Business Administration, Political Science and Public Administration were irrelevant when it comes to ministry. I therefore felt I needed advance Theological Studies because as the Mission Supervisor of the Christian Methodist Episcopal Church in Ghana, I served as the Bishop's Deputy in many capacities in Ghana by consulting and dialoguing with other denominational heads. In fact I had several opportunities to interact with Church leaders of different denominations at conferences, seminars and in some cases I represented the General Secretary of the Christian Council at Church Conferences that he couldn't attend because of his tight schedules.

Through these experiences, I realized that advance studies in Theology will help me serve the Lord better. So I made a vow to the Lord that if he grants me the opportunity to study in Seminary for the Master of Divinity degree, I will serve him better. The Lord heard my prayer and my vow. Soon, He made a way for me to study on a Scholarship for three years at the Interdenominational Theological Center in Atlanta Georgia.

That is how I ended up in Seminary in August in the Fall of 1995 in Atlanta Georgia.

My first Semester in Seminary was very exciting. I made friends from all the Major Denominations that were part of this Seminary: the United Methodist Church, the Presbyterian Church of USA, the Baptist denomination, Church of God in Christ, the

African Methodist Episcopal Church, the Christian Methodist Episcopal Church and students from other minor denominations. We attended classes together, had the same Professors teaching us, we dined together at the dinning Hall and participated together in social activities and Community work. It is a great experience to study and interact with students from these different denominations. It made us understand each other's basic Church Doctrine and Church Polity and we respected each other. Funny thing is that I had a friend from the Baptist denomination in some of the classes I took and he liked me so much that during Christmas break, he hired me in his Pet Control business to make some money during the break. In the Spring of 1996, I applied for more funds from my denomination in order to bring my family to join me. It was granted and my family joined me during the 1996 Olympic Games held in Atlanta, Georgia in the Summer. My son Samuel was almost six and was ready to start first grade when he arrived. My other son Andrew was a year and two months old and was ready for Pre-K. I was able to move out from the Dormitory to live in a two- bedroom apartment with my family. In the Fall of 1996, the children started schooling and I bought a car to make movement easier for us.

Now my responsibility was to continue with my studies while raising a family. In addition, I was assigned to serve at the Butler Street Christian Methodist Episcopal in downtown as Associate Pastor where I taught Disciples Bible Study classes for three years and assisted the Pastor in visitation to the sick and shut-ins, taught children in the Timothy Houset after School program of the Church and participated in Sunday Worship Service.

By the Spring of 1998, I was ready to graduate from the Master of Divinity degree program in Biblical Studies and Languages. Before then, I was elected the first African President of the Students Representative Council of the Interdenominational Theological

Center. It was a one-year appointment and so in my final year in April of 1998, a new President was elected to take over from me.

On graduation day in May 1998, I had many
people come to celebrate my graduation with me.

They were from my Church, the Butler Street Christian Methodist Episcopal Church, the Ghanaian Community in Atlanta and people I had ministered to in the community through the Church's outreach programs. It was a very happy graduation day followed by a grand reception at the Interdenominational Theological Center open ground. I graduated top in Biblical Studies and Languages and was awarded a special certificate in addition to my degree Certificate. I was also awarded a cash of 500 Dollars.

My son, Samuel was very excited on my graduation day. He wore my graduation cap for pictures. He was happy to see me graduate that day. Andrew was just three years old when I graduated. He was always close to his mom and I guess in his own way, he enjoyed the occasion.

In the Fall that same year 1998, I was admitted into the Doctoral program to study for the Doctor of Ministry degree in Evangelism and Church Growth at the Interdenominational Theological Center where I graduated from the Master of Divinity program.

This program was project- based so I decided to do my project on Intercessory Prayer at the Butler Street Christian Methodist Episcopal Church where I served as Associate Pastor. My desertation was titled: "The Development, Implementation and Impact of Intercessory Prayer Ministry involving the Pastoral and Lay Leadership of Butler Street Christian Methodist Episcopal Church, Atlanta, Georgia 2001".

The ministry issue was " How can the development and implementation of an Intercessory Prayer Ministry involving the Pastoral and Lay Leadership of the Church, who come together regularly under the Power of the Holy Spirit in prayer of petition and intercession, impact the life of Butler Street Christian Methodist Episcopal Church and it's ministries?".

It was a two- year project involving members of the Church who were divided into prayer groups with specific prayer topics to pray about at prayer meetings. These were vibrant prayer groups with prayer leaders directing and leading the groups in prayer at specific times of the day. The results after two years, were amazing. The Prayer Ministry taught many members how to pray effectively, enhanced the belief in the power of prayer, bonded members of the ministry in true fellowship and love, proved that Intercessory Prayer works to transform lives, and many more.

Just as I was in my final semester in the Spring of 2001, I was appointed to pastor a new Church called the Ghana Interdenominational Church made up of Ghanaian immigrants in Atlanta, Georgia.

I assumed my pastoral duties at this Church in January 2000 and graduated in May 2001 from the Doctoral program with the Doctor of Ministry degree from the Interdenominational Theological Center, Atlanta, Georgia.

After pastoring the new Church for one year, I established a new Church in Atlanta called the Friendship International Church in January 2002 to serve international immigrants from Africa and the Caribbean. I pastored this Church for twelve years from 2002-2014.

Meanwhile, in 2010, I ran for Bishop for the Christian Methodist Episcopal Church for the African work but did not win because of politics at the Conference. I continued with my ministry in the Friendship International Church and also served as Director for the International Pastoral Leadership Development Incorporated to train Church leaders in Africa for effective ministry till 2019 when I was appointed Senior Pastor for Wesley United Methodist Church in Arlington Texas.

CHAPTER 8

Summary of Pastoral Work in the USA

My Pastoral work in the United States of America started the year I arrived in the USA a second time in 1995. My first time in the USA was in 1980 when I came as a student and studied for five years at the University of Texas at Tyler and returned to Ghana in 1986 to serve the Christian Methodist Episcopal Church and the Christian Council of Ghana in Pastoral and Publishing work. This second time, I was deeply involved in studying Theology, Church Growth, Biblical Studies and Languages, Church History, Christian Education, Homiletics, and Pastoral Care and Counseling at the Interdenominational Theological Center in Atlanta Georgia.

From 1996-2001, I was studying and pastoring as Associate Pastor of Butter Street Christian Methodist Episcopal Church, From Fall 2000- December 2001, I served as Pastor of the Ghana Interdenominational Church in Decatur, Georgia.

From January 2002- 2012, I served as Senior Pastor of the Friendship International Church in Atlanta Georgia and from January 2013 - 2018, I headed the International Pastoral Leadership Development Inc. as the Director.

Throughout all this time, I published many Christian articles in the Christian Index addressing various theological issues and three major books on Prayer and Church History. In addition, I trained many African pastors from Ghana, Zimbabwe, Democratic Republic of Congo, Nigeria, Kenya and Tanzania online for effective ministry in Africa. While serving in this position, I received a call in September 2018 from some leaders of Wesley United Methodist Church in Arlington Texas inviting me to meet a search Committee for Pastor for an interview for an open Pastoral position in the Church.

I was reluctant to go because I had other plans. But upon been urged to go check things out by the Holy Spirit, I traveled to Texas to meet the Committee and to check what was going on in the Church. A couple of months later in December 2918, I received a that I have been appointed the new Pastor of Wesley United Methodist Church in Arlington Texas and should report for duty immediately.

The process was not easy. Coming from the Christian Methodist Episcopal Church Denomination to the United Methodist Church Denomination, I had to get a letter of recommendation and transfer from my Presiding Bishop and Presiding Elder, pass a background check, a phycological test, and Sexual Ethics test in order to get appointed. By God's grace, I met every requirement and on January 1, 2019, I was appointed the Senior Pastor of Wesley United Methodist Church in Arlington Texas.

I have already given details of my work in the various Churches I served from 1995-2018 in Atlanta Georgia for a span of 23 years. Now I will concentrate on my work at Wesley United Methodist Church in Arlington Texas.

Wesley United Methodist Church in Arlington Texas was the offshoot of Aldergate United Methodist Church which was organized in 1954 to the Arlington area. It operated until the 2010s when membership began to dwindle because of old age. Meanwhile, another mission Church made up of Africans started worshipping in the Fellowship Hall of the Church. While it was growing fast, the Alderga United Methodist Church was dying because of dwindled membership.

In 2014, Aldergate United Methodist Church decided to finally close it's doors. The Church worshipping in the Fellowship Hall decided to be an Uncharted mission of the United Methodist Church Denomination and the Church building of Aldergate was transferred to the new Church– Wesley United Methodist Church which operated till 2019 when I was appointed the new pastor. I am the second Pastor to serve this Church and have already served for four years. The ministry in the Church is strong in various areas of the life of Church. I have published two new books to help my congregation grow in faith and in righteousness: "Short Sermons from the New Testament" in 2021 and "Short Study of the Old Testament" in 2022. This year 2023, I have introduced new ministries to grow the Church further in the areas of Health, Food Distribution, Clothing ministry and the Music ministry.

The future of Wesley United Methodist Church in Arlington Texas is bright for Church growth. By the grace and mercy of God, the Church will flourish in the years ahead.

In addition, I started a mission work in Ghana West Africa. I visited Ghana in September 2019 after living in the United States of America for twenty four years to meet friends and relatives that have not seen me all these years. I had the opportunity to visit my village Bano-Kpezie in the Upper West Region of Ghana to preach and teach Pastors and Leaders of the Methodist Church in Ghana in that area. As a result of my visit, a new Church– Dr. Yenn-Batah United Gospel Church was organized in December 2021 in Bano-Kpezie, my hometown, with a starting membership of eighty-six in my eighteen bedroom house. I am building a new three- hundred seating capacity Church on a fifteen-acres of land donated by the Elders of my father's family for worship and educational purposes. We plan to build an Academy to educate the children in the village and a housing project for rent to support the work of the new Church.

Both Wesley United Methodist Church in Arlington Texas and Dr. Yenn-Batah United Gospel Church in Ghana have great potential in the future to win souls for Jesus Christ for the transformation of the world to the glory and honor of the Lord. We hope for great things to unfold in the years ahead. To this effect, a new and trained Pastor was appointed to lead the Church in Bano, Ghana on October 1, 2022. Glory be to God!

Throughout my life and ministry, I have allowed the Holy Spirit to lead and empower me to be fruitful and faithful in every assignment given to me. When a person is led by Holy Spirit, he reveals to you step by step what he wants you to do and demands total obedience to fulfill the purpose. When challenges come the Holy Spirit empowers you to overcome. Perhaps, after reading my life story, you are wondering how you can receive and be led by the Holy Spirit in your life. Well, the next Chapters will give you the answer and more.

CHAPTER 9

How to be Born Again

One cannot receive the Holy Spirit unless one is born again. It is a subject that Jesus Christ discussed with Nicodemus in the Gospel of John Chapter 3:1-15.

The first time Nicodemus is mentioned in the Gospel of John, he is identified as a Pharisee who come to Jesus at night.

According to the scripture, Jesus went to Jerusalem for the Passover feast. While there, he chased the money changers from the temple and overturned their tables (Mark 11:12-17). His disciples remembered then the words of Psalm 69:9 which says " Zeal for your house will consume me".

After these events, " many believed in his name when they saw the signs that he was doing" (John 2:23-25). When Nicodemus visited Jesus, he made reference to these events " Rabbi, we know that you are a teacher who has come from God. For no one could perform the signs you are doing if God were not with him"(John 3:2).

Jesus replied: "Unless one is born again he cannot see the kingdom of God" (John 3:5). Then followed a conversation with Nicodemus about the meaning of being "born again" or born from above".

Nicodemus explored the notion of being literally born again from one's mother's womb. "You cannot mean that a man is to enter the second time into his mother's womb, and be born again. Jesus expressed surprise that a teacher of Israel does not understand the concept of spiritual rebirth.

Even today, when we speak about being born again, many people like Nicodemus get confused. They don't understand that being born again is a spiritual rebirth. The Bible uses "birth" as a metaphor to describe the impartation of God's life to the sinner.

Without this life, we are otherwise dead in our sins, we follow the world and Satan, and live for our own desires (Ephesians 2:1-3). In this way, we are under the wrath of God and because of our sin, we deserve to be eternally separated from God (Romans 6:23).

But thank God that he took on human form and died in our place, taking the punishment that we deserve (Romans 5:8, 2 Corinthians 5:2).

By this, God promises forgiveness of sins and eternal life in heaven to all who receive by grace through faith, Jesus Christ the the Savior (John 1:12, 3:16, 5:24; Acts of Apostles 16:31).

Salvation is not about certain steps that we must follow. It is true that Christians must be baptized to publicly confess Christ as Savior, turn from our sins, and commit our lives to obeying God. However, these are not steps to salvation. They are results of salvation. Because of our sins, we cannot in any sense earn salvation. We could follow

many steps, and it would not be enough. "For it is by grace you have been saved, through faith– and this is not from yourselves, it is a gift of God– not by your works least any man should boast" (Ephesians 2:8-9). This is why Jesus had to die in our place. We are absolutely incapable of paying our sin debt to God or cleaning ourselves from sin. Only God could accomplish our salvation, and so He did.

Salvation and forgiveness of sins , therefore, is not about following steps. It's about receiving Jesus Christ as Savior and recognizing that He has done all of the work for us. The question to you is : Have you received Jesus Christ as your personal Savior?. If you haven't, repent of your sins, confess Him as your Savior and you will be saved. Then you will receive the Holy Spirit to guide you in your life.

" If you confess with your mouth the Lord Jesus Christ and believe in your heart that God raised Him from the dead, you will be saved. For with the heart one believes into righteousness, and with the mouth confession is made unto salvation"

(Romans 10: 9-10).

Here is further explanation of what Salvation is about. God's purpose for us is for us to experience peace and eternal life.

The Bible says: " We have peace with God

through our Lord Jesus Christ" (Romans 5:1). "For God so love the world that he gave his only begotten Son, that whosoever believes in him should not perish but have eternal life" (John3:16).

And John 10:10 tells us " I (Jesus) have come that they may have life and that they may have it more abundantly".

Yet, there is something that always prevents us from having the life that God planned for us and that is SIN. Sin separates us from God. The Bible says God created us in his own image (Genesis 1:26-28). He gave us a will and the freedom of choice but we chose to disobey Him and go our own way–which is sin. This sin is what has separated us from God. Romans 3:23 tells us: " For all have sin and fall short of the glory of God" and " The wages of sin is death,but the gift of God is eternal life in Christ Jesus our Lord"

(Romans 6:23).

Our choice to sin, therefore, has separated us from God. Unfortunately, people have tried many ways to bridge this gap between themselves and God to no avail.

Proverbs 14:12 warns us "There is a way that appears to be right, but the end leads to death". And Isaiah 59:2 tells us: " But your iniquities have separated you from God; your sins have hidden his face from you, so that he will not hear".

In order to bridge the gap of separation, God has provided us with his bridge which is the Cross. This means no other bridge reaches God except one – the Cross. Jesus died on the Cross and rose from the grave. When he did, he paid the penalty for our sin and bridged the gap between us and God. The Bible says: " For there is one God and one mediator between God and mankind, the man Jesus Christ"

(1 Timothy 2:5). " For Christ also suffered once for sins, the righteous for the unrighteous, to bring you to God" (1 Peter 3:18). This means God has provided the only way back to Him. We must therefore make a choice. The choice we make is our response to this gift of God. Our response then is to trust and receive Jesus Christ as Lord and Savior.

In John 1:12, we are told that "Yet to all who did receive receive Him, to those who believed in his name, he gave the right to become children of God".

If therefore you want to become a child of God today, you must declare with your mouth that Jesus is Lord. The Bible says "If you declare with your mouth, ,"Jesus is Lord", and believe in your heart that God raised him from the dead, you will be saved" (Romans 10:9).

If you are not saved, why don't you receive Christ as your personal Savior today?

Admit that you are a sinner.

Repent of your sins.

Believe that Jesus Christ died for you on the cross and rose from the grave.

Through prayer, invite Jesus Christ to control your life through the Holy Spirit.

You can pray this simple prayer to receive Jesus Christ into your life:

Dear God Almighty, I confess that I am a sinner and ask for your forgiveness. I believe that Jesus Christ is your Son. I believe that he died for my sin and that you raised him to life. I want to trust Him as my Savior and to follow Him as my Lord from this day forward. Guide me and help me to do your will everyday in the name of Jesus. Amen.

After this prayer, the next step is to find a Bible believing Church to join and start your Christian life. The Pastor will help you with the process to become a faithful Christian through baptism and Christian teachings. Praise the Lord that you are saved.

So we go back to Nicodemus' question about how to be born again. To be born again means to have a personal faith in Jesus as Lord and Savior and to confess Him as such. It means to be converted

(John 3:3).

CHAPTER 10

How to Receive the Baptism of the Holy Spirit

Receiving the baptism of the Holy Spirit is not something I carefully prepared for in my life to receive. I was ignorant about it and nobody taught me anything about it. All I knew is that when God called me out of the Army to attend High School for a special work, I obeyed and followed his command. By being obedient to the will of God, I believe God took steps to lead me in the path of preparation for the assignment ahead which includes being born again and receiving the baptism of the Holy Spirit.

Therefore, the baptism of the Holy Spirit that I received while in Bible College was to prepare me for ministry and it was by the grace and mercy of God.

If you are seeking the baptism of the Holy Spirit, your case may be different from mine. To guide you therefore, I think you need some preparation. The first thing you must have before asking for the baptism of the Holy Spirit is the right motive. Some people may want it because their friends have it or their Church members have it, or they want to speak in tongues, or they want God's power in order to be able to do their own will, use the gifts to build riches for themselves or their empires rather than what God's will is for their lives.

Don't desire the baptism of the Holy Spirit and the gifts for your own selfish purpose but rather desire it for what God wants to do with your life. Desire the gift in order to draw closer to God the Father, Son and the Holy Spirit to build your own personal relationship with God. What God wants from each one of us is an intimate personal relationship. Therefore, once we receive this gift, we will be able to draw closer to God.

The other reason we must desire this gift is to receive God's super natural power to flow through us so that we can accomplish whatever God's perfect will is going to be for our lives.

The gift of the baptism of the Holy Spirit is only for people who want to go all out for God. If God is going to release the Holy Spirit into our soul area, then he is going to want us to do something with it. He has specific plan and destiny for each person's life. Therefore if he releases the Holy Spirit into our lives, we will have God's power available to do what he wants to do with our lives. If we are not willing to be used by God for whatever he wants to use us for in this life, then this gift of anointing is just going to be wasted and God will more likely withhold it from us. This means that we must understand the ramifications and the responsibility that comes from receiving this gift. If we are not ready and willing to go all out for the Lord in this life, then we will be wasting our time asking for it.

Having, therefore, the right motive and really wanting this gift will be the main determining factors as to whether or not we receive it when we ask for it.

The third important factor to consider apart from having the right motive and really wanting this gift is total surrender to God.

The baptism of the Holy Spirit and the gift that accompany it entails that we will be willing to fully surrender to whatever God's perfect plan and destiny is going to be for our life. The four areas that we need to surrender are our body, soul, spirit and our entire life. When God calls us, he wants to sanctify us completely in all parts of our beings and he wants our entire life to be dedicated to him. If we are not willing to make a full and complete surrender of our body, soul, spirit and our entire life over to him, then we will probably not receive this gift from God.

Lastly, if we are ready to receive this gift, we must confess all our sins because just as we want Christ to come to a "clean house", so it is with the Holy Spirit. Once we confess our sins, we can then ask for the baptism of the Holy Spirit.

In my case, I received it when I was in Bible College at a prayer meeting. I don't know in what context or circumstances you will receive it but surely, it will be when you draw closer to God in prayer, repentance, confession, and supplication.

"I baptize you with water for repentance, but he who is coming after me is mightier than I, whose sandals I am not worthy to carry; he will baptize you with the Holy Spirit and with fire" (Matthew 3:11). The baptism of the Holy Spirit comes after we have confessed Jesus Christ as our Lord and Savior and have been baptized by water. In theology, we say justification first followed by sanctification.

Justification means to be made righteous in the sight of God and Sanctification means to be set apart for God's special use. The baptism of the Holy Spirit sets us apart for God to use us according to his plan for our lives.

May the Lord favor you with the baptism of the Holy Spirit so that you can receive extraordinary gift of power to use for His service.

CHAPTER 11

How to be Led by the Holy Spirit

After the baptism of the Holy Spirit, we must be led by the Holy Spirit in all we do. Jesus is our example. After he was baptized by the Holy Spirit, he was led into the wilderness to fast and pray (Luke 4:1). After that, he began his ministry full of power and grace. Throughout his life, Jesus was led by the Holy Spirit and so must we when we are baptized by the Holy Spirit.

From my experience, if you want to be led by the Holy Spirit, you must constantly be obedient to the Holy Spirit in all things. The work of the Holy Spirit in the believer are numerous. The Holy Spirit regenrates us, Regeneration is the impartation of life, spiritual life to the one who is "dead in trespasses and sin" (Ephesians 2:1).

The Holy Spirit also sets those of us in Christ free from the law of sin and death. There are many Christians who live in their own strength, wisdom and by the law.

The law does not set us free. The law traps us and imprisons us in guilt and sin. But the Holy Spirit sets us free from the law and bondage. It is the work of the Holy Spirit- when we give up trying to live right in our own strength and surrender- to help us walk in the power of the Holy Spirit and to set us free from this awful law of sin and death.

The Holy Spirit strengthens us with power in the inward man. In Ephesians 3:16, we are told that " he would grant you, according to his riches of his glory, that ye may be strengthened with power through his Spirit in the inward man".

Other works of the Holy Spirit are to guide us into holy living as children of God, to lead godlike life, to bear witness together with our spirit that we are the children of God, to help us bear the fruit of the Spirit

The Guidance of the Holy Spirit

(Galatians 5:22), to guide us into all the truth, to help us remember the words of Jesus and to reveal to us the deep things of God which are hidden from the natural man.

There are other works of the Holy Spirit in our lives that are very important too but suffice it to say that the Holy Spirit demands total surrender of our lives to him in order to experience the manifestation of his power in our lives.

To be led by the Holy Spirit therefore, we need to follow His guidance. In addition to yielding to His conviction, we also need to become aware of the Holy Spirit's leading by reading the Bible and by praying.

In Galatians 5:16-18, the Apostle Paul tells us to "walk in the Spirit, and you will not gratify the desires of the flesh. For the flesh desires what is contrary to the Spirit, and the Spirit what is contrary to the flesh. They are in conflict with each other, so that you are not to do whatever you want. But if you are led by the Spirit, you are not under the law".

To be led by the Spirit, therefore, means that when we place our faith in Christ and confess Him as our Lord and Savior, we are given the Holy Spirit to permanently indwell us and He never leaves us. The Lord Jesus Christ referred to the Holy Spirit as "the Helper" (John 14:26). He is referred to as "the Helper" because He helps us in our struggle against temptations, the flesh and the devil. Even when we don't know what to pray for, the Holy Spirit intercedes with moans and groans that words cannot express (Roman 8:26).

In times of our lives when we feel overwhelmed with sorrow, pain, and grief, the Holy Spirit intervenes on our behalf and communicates our feelings to the Father. In addition to intervening on our behalf and guiding us, the Holy Spirit also leads us if we allow Him to do so.

Being led by the Holy Spirit is a popular topic today among Christians and in Churches but many do not know what it really means to be led by the Holy Spirit. When the Apostle Paul tells us to be " led by the Spirit", he is referring to the fact that we should be open and receptive of the Holy Spirit's guidance. Indeed, what the Holy Spirit wants from us is for us to do the right things in life and to avoid sin. When we commit sin, the Holy Spirit convicts our hearts and minds so that through the conviction of the Holy Spirit, we can repent and turn back to God.

Unfortunately, if we consistently refuse to listen to the Holy Spirit's guidance and conviction, we can become cold and callous to the Spirit's guidance. When this happens, we cannot be " led by the Holy Spirit". Instead, we will be led by our sinful flesh. It is therefore, very important for believers in Christ Jesus to follow after God and obey the Holy Spirit's convictions and guidance. It is only when we listen to the Holy Spirit's convictions and guidance that we can truly say we are "led by the Spirit".

When we choose to follow the Holy Spirit, then we are not walking in accordance with the flesh (Galatians 5:16-18).

It is important for us to always remember that our sinful flesh and the Holy Spirit are both constantly in conflict inside of us and this can be troubling for us because oftentimes, it is easier for us to follow our sinful flesh rather than the guidance of the Holy Spirit and following the Holy Spirit is always the right thing to do. If we allow the Holy Spirit to lead us, we will grow in our relationship in Christ as well as grow in Christian maturity. Much as it is hard to follow the lead of the Holy Spirit, it is completely worth it to follow the lead of the Holy Spirit in our lives. I encourage you to take an active decision to follow the lead of the Holy Spirit rather than your sinful flesh.

In my walk with the Holy Spirit, every decision that I took on my own without the guidance of the Holy Spirit, turned out to be a disaster in my life and the consequences have been unpleasant. Sometimes, I wish I had obeyed the Holy Spirit's guidance and counsel but it is too late..

Lastly, l want to stress that when we are led by the Holy Spirit, we will produce the fruit of the Spirit in our lives as mentioned in Galatians 5:22-23. " But the fruit of the Spirit is love, joy, peace, forbearance, kindness, goodness, faithfulness, gentleness and self-control. Against such things there is no law".

The fruit of the Spirit is what God wants to cultivate in our lives and we cannot produce these fruits if we are not led by the Holy Spirit. The opposite is that we will produce the acts of the flesh: " sexual immorality, impurity, debauchery, idolatry and witchcraft, hatred, discord, jealousy, fits of rage, selfish ambition, dissentions, factions and envy, drunkenness, orgies and the like" (Galatians 5:19-22).

We can distinguish what kind of life we are leading based on our actions, thought patterns, and behavior. If we are cultivating and producing the fruit of the Spirit in our lives, then we are truly being led by the Holy Spirit and we are walking in accordance with His will.

On the other hand, if we see the deeds of the sinful flesh being cultivated and produced in our lives, then we are following the lead of our flesh and we are walking in accordance with our sinful nature.

The good news is that if we find ourselves being led by our sinful flesh rather than the Holy Spirit, we can change direction by asking God to help us be more sensitive to the Holy Spirit's convictions, guidance, and revelation in order to cultivate the fruit of the Holy Spirit in our lives.

We must always remember that throughout our lives, we will constantly be challenged to follow the leading of the Holy Spirit or the leading of our sinful nature. This challenge is hard but with the help of God, we can follow the Holy Spirit's lead throughout our lives and bring glory and honor to God.

CHAPTER 12

Biblical People Led by the Holy Spirit

In order to inspire us to walk in the Spirit, let us look at some saints in the Bible who walked in the Spirit and how it made a difference in their lives. The Bible makes it clear that there are two kinds of life and two ways to live. We are either in the flesh or in the Spirit according to Romans Chapter 8:9. We can walk according to the flesh or according to the Spirit (Galatians 5:25). This means the sinner lives in the flesh and walks according to the flesh. But the Christian is in the Spirit and ideally walks after the Spirit. Yet there are many Christians and saints walking after the flesh. Walking in the ways of the flesh is very abnormal for believers and we must do our best to submit our lives to the Holy Spirit to help us walk after the Spirit.

Fortunately, there are many Biblical examples of people who walked in the Spirit to inspire us.. Let us look at a few examples.

*****Jesus is our best model of a life lived in step with the Holy Spirit. But Jesus is not the only one who walked in the Spirit. The Bible clearly gives us more examples of individuals who walked in the Spirit. As we look at the lives of these individuals, their lives should give us a picture of how life is meant to be. Their lives define what is normal and exposes the poverty of life lived according to the flesh. The kind of life they lived is what can be described as the abundant life in John 10:10. Their lives therefore, must inspire us to live a life in the Spirit.

*"****The first person we shall look at is Simeon.

In Like 2:21-32, we read:. " On the eighth day, when it was time to circumcise him, he was named Jesus, the name the angel had given him before he had been conceived. When the time of purification according to the Law of Moses had been completed, Joseph and Mary took him to Jerusalem to present him to the Lord as it is written in the Law of the Lord. 'Every firstborn male is to be consecrated to the Lord; and to offer a sacrifice in keeping with what is said in the Law of the Lord: a pair of doves or two young pigeons'.

Now there was a man in Jerusalem called Simeon, who was righteous and devout. He was waiting for the consolation of Israel, and the Holy Spirit was upon him. It had been revealed to him by the Holy Spirit that he would not die before he had seen the Lord's Christ. Moved by the Spirit, he went into the temple courts. When the parents brought the child Jesus to do for him what the custom of the Law required, Simeon took him in his arms and Praised God saying:

" Sovereign Lord, as you have promised, now dismiss your servant in peace.

For my eyes have seen your salvation, which you have prepared in the sight of people, a light for revelation to the Gentiles and for glory to your people Israel".

For hundreds of years, the prophets had been straining to see the promised Messiah. Then Simeon, moved by the Holy Spirit, goes to the temple courts and sees what the other prophets had missed.

There is no doubt that those who are led by the Holy Spirit are always at the right place at the right time. Wouldn't it be wonderful if we allowed the Holy Spirit to lead us always to the right places at the right time in our lives? Yes that can happen only if we are led by the Holy Spirit.

,*****The next is Peter and John. They declared the Gospel boldly in the face of persecution. In Acts of Apostles Chapter 4:8-12, we see how the Holy Spirit led and emboldened these uneducated people to declare boldly the gospel in the face of persecution.

" Then Peter, filled with the Holy Spirit, said to them,: "Rulers and elders of the people! If we are being called to account today for an act of kindness shown to a man who was lame and are being asked how he was healed, then know this, you and all the people of Israel: It is by the name of Jesus Christ of Nazareth whom you crucified but whom God raised from the dead, that this man stands healed. Jesus is "the stone that you builders rejected, which has become the cornerstone". Salvation is found in no one else, for there is no other name under heaven given to mankind by which we must be saved".

When we are led by the Holy Spirit, we receive power and boldness to preach the gospel and to defend the gospel in the face of persecution and that is exactly what we see in the life of Peter and John in this passage.

*****Another example is Stephen. In Acts of Apostles Chapter 6, we read about Stephen who was one of the seven deacons chosen to serve tables. The Bible says he was a man full of grace and power who worked great signs among the people. But some of the people belonging to the various groups and synagogues arose and disputed with him. "But they could not stand against the wisdom the Spirit gave him as he spoke" (Acts of Apostles Chapter 6:10).

In the case of Stephen, we learn that those who are led by the Holy Spirit and serve in newness of the Spirit, will encounter opposition from those who persist in the oldness of the Law (Torah). There will be arguments, and one could die from persecution just like Jesus, Paul, Peter, Stephen et all. But no weapon formed against us will prosper and we will refute every judgmental and critical tongue that arises in opposition to the message of Christ and his finished work because we are filled with the Holy Spirit.

So far, we have looked at some Biblical examples of people who walked in the Holy Spiri: Simeon, Peter and John, and Stephen. There are more.

******Barnabas. "But Barnabas took him and brought him to the apostles. He told them how Saul on his journey had seen the

Lord and that the Lord had spoken to him, and how in Damascus he had preached fearlessly in the name of Jesus"

(Acts 9:27). Though the apostles were all filled with the Holy Spirit, only Barnabas was led by the e Spirit to speak on behalf of Saul now Paul. None of the Apostles trusted the man once known as Saul. They regarded him from a worldly point of view and were afraid of him. But Barnabas took him and brought him to the apostles. Barnabas saw what no one else saw and through one act of encouragement, helped changed the course of Church history. It all happened because Barnabas was very extraordinary in being sensitive to the leading of the Holy Spirit. Are you like Barnabas?

*****The Apostle Paul led by the Holy Spirit, was able to write down the doctrine of a new covenant. First, Jesus revealed the grace of God for a sinful world and Paul wrote it down so we wouldn't forget it. In 1 Corinthians 2:13, we see Paul preaching a message that went against everything he had learned in the Pharisee school. We all know that he had been trained in the old ways of the written code but he began to serve in the new ways seen in Romans 7:6. "But now, by dying to what once bound us, we have been released from the Law so that we serve in the new way of the Spirit, and not in the old way of the written code". Those who are led by the Spirit, have a "competence that comes from God".

"He made us competent as ministers of a new covenant— not of the letter but of the Spirit, for the letter kills but the Spirit gives life" (2 Corinthians 3:6).

In addition to this, Paul, led by the Holy Spirit in his second missionary journey, went to Macedonia instead of Brithynia because he received a vision to go to Macedonia. As a result of this, the Philippians got the gospel and we have the joy-filled letter to the Philippians in the Bible. Led by the Holy Spirit, Paul also went to Jerusalem in spite of the hardship he knew waited for him. Those who live in the Spirit, walk fearlessly into the toughest and most hostile places on earth for God never leaves us when he sends us to places we are not sure of our security.

There are many more examples of people in the Bible who were led by the Holy Spirit that we haven't discussed but suffice us to say the few examples given above should encourage us to walk in the Spirit in order to fulfill God's purposes for our lives.

CHAPTER 13

The Holy Spirit in the Old Testament

One of the mistakes most believers make is to assume that the Holy Spirit's activity in Scripture is limited to the Synoptic Gospels: Matthew 3:13-17, Mark 1:9-11, and Luke 3:21-23 in the New Testament starting with these verses:

"As soon as Jesus was baptized, he went out of the water. At that moment heaven opened, and he saw the Spirit of God descending like a dove and alighting on him. And a voice from heaven said, This is my Son, whom I love, with him I am well pleased" (Matthew 3 16-17).

But the truth is that the Holy Spirit is just as active in the Old Testament as in the New Testament.. In this chapter, I willl explore the work of the Holy Spirit in the Old Testament for our understanding of Scripture.

In Isaiah 42:1-9, we see the intimate interworking of the triune God– Father, Son and the Holy Spirit– especially the Spirit's powerful role found in the Old Testament. The passage summarizes the redeeming work of all three persons of the Trinity in the salvation of the lost. It helps us to understand how the passage ties together in remarkable harmony both in the Old Testament and the New Testament, the understanding of God's grace and it sheds light on our understanding of the Holy Spirit.

Here are some examples of the work of the Holy Spirit in the Old Testament.

The Holy participated in creation as seen in Genesis 1:1-2, Job 26:13, and Isaiah 32:15. " In the beginning God created the heavens and the earth. Now the earth was formless and empty, darkness was over the surface of the deep, and the SPIRIT of God was hovering over the waters" (Genesis 1:1-2).

The Spirit gives life to humanity and other creatures. " When you hide your face, they are terrified, when you take away their breath, they die and return to dust. When you send the SPIRIT, they are created, and you renew the face of the ground" (Psalm 194: 29-39).

The Spirit strives with sinners in Genesis 6:3 which is related to his

work in the New Testament in John 16:8-11.

" Then the Lord said, "My SPIRIT will not contend with humans forever, for they are mortal; their days will be a hundred and twenty years" (Genesis 6:3).

" When he comes, he will prove the world to be in the wrong about sin and righteousness and judgment: about sin, because people do not believe in me; about righteousness because I am going to the Father, where you can see me no longer, and about judgment, because the prince of this world now stand condemned" (John 16:8-11).

In the Old Testament, we see the Spirit come upon certain judges, warriors, and prophets in a way that gave them extraordinary power; for example Joshua. And the Lord said to Moses, " Take Joshua son of Nun, a man in whom is the SPIRIT and lay your hand on him"(Numbers 27:18), Othniel (Judges 3:10), Gideon (Judges 6:34), Samson (Judges 13:25; 14:6), and Saul (1 Samuel 10:9-10). In the case of Saul, the Spirit later departed from him because of his disobedience (1 Samuel 16:14).

The Spirit also played a prominent role in the long span of Old Testament prophecy. David declared that " the Spirit of the Lord spoke by me, and His word was on my tongue"(2 Samuel 23:2).

Likewise Ezekiel reported that " the Spirit entered me when He spoke to me"(Ezekiel 2:2).

In Psalm 143:10, we see the Spirit inspired holiness in the Old Testament.

" Teach me to do your will,

for you are my God,
may your good Spirit
lead me on level ground".

In addition, in Ezekiel 36:27,we read about the promise that someday God would put His Spirit in His people in a way that would cause them to live according to His statutes.

The Spirit was very crucial in helping God's people to prepare for the coming ministry of the Messiah. For example, Isaiah 11:1-5 is a preview of the work of the Father, the Holy Spirit and the Son who is a branch of Jesse.

Looking forward to the ministry of the
Lord Jesus Christ, the Holy Spirit inspired Isaiah to prophecy;
" The Spirit the Lord shall rest upon Him"(Isaiah 12:2). The Holy Spirit also inspired the Chosen one with wisdom, understanding, counsel,
might, knowledge, fear of the Lord, righteousness and faithfulness.

This brings us to full cycle to the New Testament where Jesus claimed to be the fulfillment of prophecy (Isaiah 61: 1-2; and Luke 4:18-19).

" The Spirit of the Lord is upon me,
because he has anointed me to
proclaim good news to the poor,
He has sent me to proclaim
freedom for the prisoners and
recovering of sight for the blind,
to set the oppressed free, to
proclaim the year of the Lord's
favor" (Luke 4:18-19).

Therefore,as we can see from the Old Testament, the Holy Spirit was active in creation, in the life of prophets, warriors and judges long before manifesting in the New Testament with the baptism of Jesus by John the Baptist at the River Jordan,

The Guidance of the Holy Spirit

" As soon as Jesus was baptized he went up out of the water. At that moment heaven was opened and he saw the Spirit of the Lord descending like a dove and alighting on him. And a voice from heaven said; "This is my Son, whom I love; with him I am well pleased".(Matthew 4:16-17).

When we study the manifestation of the Holy Spirit in the life of our Lord Jesus Christ, we will find that everything he did on earth was done by the power of the Holy Spirit. We too, can be led by the Holy Spirit if we are blessed with the baptism of the Holy Spirit.

Here are some of the works of the Holy Spirit in the life of Jesus.

******Jesus was begotten of the Holy Spirit. " And the angel answered and said unto her, The Holy Spirit shall come upon you, and the power of the Most High shall overshadow you; therefore also that holy thing which shall be born of you shall be called the Son of God" (Luke 1:35).

******Jesus Christ led a holy, spotless life, and offered Himself to God , through the working of the Holy Spirit. " The Spirit of the Lord is upon me, because he has anointed me to preach the gospel to the poor, he has sent me to heal the brokenhearted, to preach deliverance to the captives, and recovery of sight to the blind, to set at liberty them that are bruised"(Luke 4:18). " How God anointed Jesus of Nazareth with the Holy Spirit and with power; who went about doing good, and healing all that were oppressed of the devil; for God was with him" (Acts 10:38).

****** Jesus Christ was anointed for service by the Holy Spirit. "And Jesus Christ being full of the Holy Spirit, returned from Jordan and was led by the Spirit into the wilderness" (Luke 4:1).

*******Jesus Christ was taught by the Spirit who rested upon Him. The Spirit was the source of His wisdom in the days of His flesh. " And I knew him not: but he that sent me to baptize with water, the same said unto me, Upon whom thou shall see the Spirit descending and remaining on him, the same is he which baptizes with the Holy Spirit" (John 1:35).

******Jesus Christ was led by the Holy Spirit in His movements. " And the Spirit of the Lord shall rest upon him, the spirit of wisdom and understanding, the spirit of counsel and might, the spirit of knowledge and of the fear of the Lord" (Isaiah 11:2).

******* The Holy Spirit abode upon Him in fulnes and the words He spoke were the words of God. " For he whom God has sent speaks the word of God: for he gives not the Spirit by measure" (John 3:34).

******* Jesus Christ gave commandments to His apostles whom he had chosen, through the Holy Spirit. " Until the day in which he was taken up, after that he through the Holy Spirit gave command to the apostles whom he had chosen"

(Acts 1:2).

******Jesus Christ did his miracles in the power of the Holy Spirit. " But if I cast out devil's by the Spirit of God, then the Kingdom of God is come to you" (Matthew 12: 28).

*******Jesus Christ was raised from the dead by the power of the Holy Spirit. " But if the Spirit of Him that raised up Jesus from the dead dwell in you, he that raised up Christ from the dead shall also quicken your mortal bodies by his Spirit that dwells in you" (Romans 8:11).

These are a few examples of how the Holy Spirit worked in the life of Jesus Christ when he manifested in the flesh.

We can also allow the Holy Spirit to manifest in our lives if we submit to the power of the Holy Spirit. In the next Chapter, I give Biblical references on being led by the Spirit. Reading these verses should motivate you to seek the guidance and leadership of the Holy Spirit in your life.

CHAPTER 14

Scripture Verses on Being Led by the Holy Spirit

In this chapter, let me give you a few Biblical passages on how to be led by the Holy Spirit. Reading these verses in your Bible should help you stay focus on your lwalk in the Spirit. All verses are from the New International Version of the Bible.

Romans 8:14 " For those who are led by the Spirit of God are the children of God".

John 16:13 " But when he, the Spirit of truth, come, he will guide you into all truth. He will not speak only what he hears, and he will tell you you what is to come".

Romans 5:5 " And hope does not put us to shame, because God's love has been poured out into our hearts through the Holy Spirit, who has been given to us".

Galatians 5:22 " But the fruit of the Spirit is love, joy, peace, forbearance, kindness, goodness, faithfulness, gentleness and self-control. Against such things there is no law".

1 John 3:24 " Those who obey his commands live in him, and he in them. And this is how we know that he lives in us: We know it by the Spirit he gave us".

1 Corinthians 12:3 " Therefore, I tell you that no one who is speaking by the Spirit of God says 'Jesus is cursed', " and no one can say, 'Jesus is Lord' except by the Holy Spirit".

1 John 3:9 " No one who is born of God will continue to sin, because God's seed remains in him,he cannot go on sinning, because he has been born of God".

2 Timothy 3:16 " All Scripture is God- breathed and is useful for teaching, rebuking, correcting and training for righteousness".

Ephesians 3:16 " I pray that out of his glorious riches he may strengthen you with power through his Spirit in your inner being".

Ephesians 5:18 " Do not get drunk on wine, which leads to debauchery. Instead, be filled with the Spirit".

Galatians 4:6 " Because you are sons, God sent the Spirit of his Son into our hearts, the Spirit who calls out ' Abba, Father".

Galatians 5:18 " But if you are led by the Spirit, you are not under the law".

John 14:26 " But the Counselor, the Holy Spirit, whom the Father will send in my name, will teach you all things and will remind you of everything I have said to you".

John 16:7 " But I tell you the truth: it is for your good that I am going away. Unless I go away, the Counselor will not come to you; but if I go, I will send him to you".

John 3:5 Jesus answered, " I tell you the truth, no one can enter the kingdom of God unless he is born of water and the Spirit".

John 3:6 " Flesh gives birth to flesh, but the Spirit gives birth to spirit".

Luke 4:1 " Jesus full of the Holy Spirit, returned from the Jordan and was led by the Spirit in the desert".

Romans 8:11 " And if the Spirit of him who raised Jesus from the dead is living in you, he who raised Christ from the dead will also give life to your mortal bodies through his Spirit who lives in you".

Romans 8:13-14 "For if you live according to the sinful nature, you will die, but if by the Spirit you put to death the misdeeds of the body, you will live; because those who are led by the Spirit of God are sons of God".

Romans 8:16 " The Spirit himself testifies with our spirit that we are the children of God".

Romans 8:9 " You, however, are controlled not by the sinful nature but by the Spirit, if the Spirit of God lives in you".

Mark 1:12 " At once the Spirit sent him out into the desert".

Isaiah 48:16 Come near to me and listen to this: " From the first announcement I have not spoken in secret; at the time it happens,

I am there. "And now the Sovereign Lord has sent me with his Spirit".

Acts 8:29 " The Spirit told Philip, "Go to that chariot and stay bear it".

Acts 10:19-20 While Peter was still thinking about the vision, the Spirit said to him, " Simon, three men are looking for you. So get up and go downstairs. Do not hesitate to go with them, for I have sent them".

Acts 13:2 While they were worshipping the Lord and fasting, the Holy Spirit said, " Set apart for me Barnabas and Saul for the work to which I have called them".

Acts 16:6 " Paul and his companions traveled throughout the region of Phrygia and Galatia, having being kept by the Holy Spirit from preaching the wording the province of Asia".

Acts 20:22 " And now compelled by the Spirit, I am going to Jerusalem, not knowing what will happen to me there".

Revelation 4:2 " At once I was in the Spirit, and there before me was a throne in heaven with someone sitting on it".

Revelation 21:10 " And he carried me away in the Spirit to a mountain great and high, and showed me the Holy City, Jerusalem, coming down out of heaven from God".

These are some of the Bible verses that can help you understand how the Holy Spirit operates and how to be led by the Holy Spirit if you receive the baptism of the Holy Spirit. I pray that the Lord will bless you as you are led by the Holy Spirit in your life.

CHAPTER 15

The Mark of a Spirit-filled Christian

Perhaps you are wondering how you can know that you are walking in the Spirit.

Well, you need to look for these characteristics in a Spirit-filled believer:

First the Spirit of Christ must rule in our lives " in order that the righteous requirement of the law might be fully met in us, who do not live according to the flesh but according to the Spirit.

Those who live according to the flesh have their minds set on what the flesh desires, but those who live in accordance with the Spirit, have their minds set on what the Spirit desires. The mind govern by the flesh is death, but the mind govern by the Spirit is life and peace" (Romans 8:4-6).

In addition, Galatians 5:16-17, 25 has this to say: " So I say, walk in the Spirit, and you will not gratify the desires of the flesh.

For the flesh desires what is contrary to the Spirit, and the Spirit what is contrary to the flesh. They are in conflict with each other, so that you are not to do whatever you want------ Since we live by the Spirit, let us keep in step with the Spirit".

A Spirit-led believer allows the Spirit of Christ to rule in his or her life.

Second, a Spirit-led life produces fruit of Christ-like character. Romans 15:13 is a prayer by the Apostle Paul to the Romans.

"May the God of hope fill you with all joy and peace as you trust in him, so that you may overflow with hope by the power of the Holy Spirit". Love, joy and peace are part of the fruit of the Spirit and Paul was praying for the believers to produce these fruits by the power of the Spirit. So must we also.

In Galatians 5:22-23, Paul lists the fruit of the Spirit for us to think about and pray that we bear the fruit of the Spirit.

"But the fruit of the Spirit is love, joy, peace, forbearance, kindness, goodness, faithfulness, gentleness and self-control. Against such things there is no law".

Third, the Spirit gives us liberty. Liberty not to sin but to live in righteousness and freedom from the desires of the flesh.

"But now, by dying to what once bound us, we have been released from the law so that we serve in the new way of the Spirit, and not in the oldest of the written code"

(Romans 7:6).

" Now the Lord is the Spirit, and where the Spirit of the Lord is, there is liberty"

(2 Corinthians 3:17).

"It is for freedom that Christ has set us free. Stand firm, then, and do not let yourselves be burden again by the yoke of slavery "(Galatians 5:1).

Fourth, the Spirit-filled life is a life of perfect contentment. Paul reminds us Philippians 4;11 " I am not saying this because I am in need, for I have learned to be content whatever the circumstances".

We can only praise God when we are perfectly content with all His dealings with us. If we believe in God who is sovereign and who can therefore make things that befall us work together for our good

(Romans 8:28), then we can be truly content in all circumstances and praise Him at all times when we are filled with the Holy Spirit. So the fourth characteristics of a person led by the Holy Spirit is contentment in all circumstances which leads to constant praising of the Lord.

Fifth, the Spirit-filled life is a life of growth in holiness. As our own life increases in holiness so does our consciousness of the holiness of God. The two go together. After twenty-five years of Paul's convertion, he could say " I am the least of the Apostles"

(1 Corinthians 25:9). The closer he walked with God, the more he was concious of the corruption of the flesh. He recognized

that no good thing could be found in the flesh (Romans 7:18). Therefore, the Spirit-filled believer does not merely seek to give the impression that he or she is growing in holiness, but is actually doing so.

Sixth, the Spirit-filled life is a life that is crucified. The Apostle Paul tells us in Galatians 2:20 that " I am crucified with Christ". This means the way of the cross is the fullness of the Holy Spirit. The Holy Spirit will always lead us just as he led Jesus Christ to the cross. The two are inseparable because the cross is a symbol of weakness, shame and death. Paul himself had fears, sorrows and perplexities in his life (2 Corinthians 1:8, 4:8, 6:10 and 7:5). All this is incongruous with the Spirit's fullness, rather the Spirit-filled believer will find God leading him or her further and further down the pathway of humiliation and death. This is the meaning of a crucified life.

Seventh, the Spirit-filled life is a life of constant enlargement. The Holy Spirit is constantly exploring to enlarge our capacity in life and ministry, so that He can fill us to a greater degree. But there can be no enlargement in our lives if we avoid the pathway of the cross.

Then he said to them all, " Whoever wants to be my disciple must deny themselves and take up their cross and follow me (Luke 9:23). If we accept the cross consistently in our lives, we shall find our cup becoming larger and large, becoming a river and the river becoming many rivers. At each stage our capacity is enlarged, we will need to be filled again and again thus fulfilling in us the promise in John 7:38 "Whoever believes in me, as the Scripture says, stream of living water will flow from within him". 2 Corinthians 3:18 reminds us that the Holy Spirit leads us from one degree of glory to another. Thus the Spirit-filled believer has great potential to constantly grow into greater dimension.

To conclude this Chapter, let me stress that there are signs that you will not find in a Spirit-filled believer.

*******A Spirit-filled believer will not necessarily be noisy, highly excited or full of physical strength. The Spirit-filled person's life is a life of calm poise, and quiet confidence (Isaiah 30:15). Oftentimes, people not filled with the Holy Spirit are the people who are noisy and display all kinds of behavior that is contrary to the gentleness of the Holy Spirit. Be careful not to fall for their deceitfulness.

********The Spirit-filled life is not a life free from temptation (1 Corinthians 19:13). Temptations will come but by the power of the Holy Spirit in us, we shall overcome.

******* To be filled with the Spirit doesn't mean we have reached a state of sinless perfection or we have attain a state where the old nature is eradicated

(1 John 1:8,10). My advise to you is: Watch and pray that you don't fall into temptation.

****"* Lastly, the Spirit-filled life is not a life where further and fuller growth is impossible or unnecessary (2 Peter 3:18).

There is always room for growth. Therefore, the Spirit-filled believer must always be open to the Holy Spirit's leading and guidance for further spiritual growth in life.

It is my prayer that these characteristics of a Spirit-filled believer will guide you as you grow into Christian maturity.

CHAPTER 16

How to Overcome Temptations

Throughout the previous chapters of this book, we have been discussing how to be born again and how to be led by the Holy Spirit in our lives. In this chapter, there is one important factor that we need to take into account if we want to be faithful in our walk in the Spirit. It is temptation. As we grow as Christians, we can only be successful if we draw closer to God.

Temptation is anything that influences us to disobey God. If we want to overcome temptation to sin, we must consider these Biblical strategies to grow in holiness before God.

As believers, we must always bear in mind that any situation we face in life will either promote our growth or promote our destruction. The determine factor is what we decide in our hearts to do. It is either we obey God and draw near to Him or rebel against God and run from Him. We can't be passive victims in this situation. Instead of choosing to sin, we must resolve to strategize in order to overcome temptations in our lives.

There are many strategies that we can apply to overcome temptations. The first is for us to be reconciled to God. The Bible makes it clear that the first step is for us to turn to God in repentance and faith. That means we must acknowledge that only Jesus the Christ can make us right before God. He died in our place to satisfy the just wrath of God against our sin and He rose from the dead to prove the debt was paid. Apart from Christ, all people are enslaved to sin. We obey sin's desires and attempt to live apart from God's righteous commandments. But " thanks be to God that, though you used to be slaves to sin, you wholeheartedly obeyed the form of teaching to which you were entrusted. You have been set free from sin and have become slaves to righteousness"(Romans 6:17-18).

As believers in Jesus Christ, we thank God that "the Lord knows how to rescue godly men from trials and to hold the unrighteous for the day of judgement" (2 Peter 2:9).

The third strategy to overcome temptation in our lives is for us to cultivate Godliness. There is so much ungodliness in our society that we are easily tempted to fall into it's grips. As long as we live, we will always be subjected to it in some aspect for temptations are very "common to man" (1 Corinthians 10:13). Therefore we need to watch ourselves. Temptation can only succeed when our heart is unprepared for it. Therefore we need to" put on the Lord Jesus and make no provision for the flesh in regard to it's lusts" (Romans 13:14).

Denying ungodly desires is not enough. We must find our godly desires and fulfill them in the Lord. Instead of looking for pleasures apart from God, " Delight yourself in the Lord, And he will give you the desires of your heart" (Psalm 37:4).

Strive against sin in your life and seek to "do all in the name of the Lord Jesus Christ" (Colossians 3:17).

Strategy number four is for us to avoid tempting situations in our lives. The Lord. Jesus in teaching the disciples to pray the Lord's prayer, taught them to ask God not to " lead us into temptation, but deliver us from the evil one" (Matthew 6:13). If we ask God to help us avoid or overcome temptations, then we must also be on our guard and stay away from tempting situations.

Proverbs 7:6-10 warns about putting ourselves in situations that will lead us to fall to temptation. This means if we find ourselves in danger of sin, we must get out of there quickly. We must always stay away from those who influence us to do evil. Psalm 1:1-2 says, " Blessed is a man who does no walk in the counsel of the wicked or stand in the way of sinners or sit in the seat of the mockers. But his delight is in the law of the Lord, and on his law he medidates day and night".As believers, we are to "flee from youthful lusts (2 Timothy 2:22), "flee immorality" (1 Corinthians 6:18). Escape from tempting situations, locations, and people. Do not yield to your ungodly desires but make every effort to subdue them for righteousness sake

(Matthew 5:29-39).

This means we might have to abandon our friendship with people who tempt us towards evil. Take your relationship seriously. "Do not be misled: " Bad company corrupts good character"

(1 Corinthians 15:33).

The fifth strategy to overcome temptations is for us to be honest with God. Sin is fundamentally directed against God. We must agree with God that sin is wicked and deserves to be punished. David the King of Israel recognized this when he committed the sin of adultery and murder.

He confessed and lamented before God,

" For I know my transgressions, and my sins is always before me. Against You, you only, I have sinned and done what is evil in Your sight, so that You are right in your verdict and justified when you judge"

(Psalm 51: 3-4). It is always very important for us to tell God about our sins and temptations because the Bible says " If we confess our sins, He is faithful and righteous to forgive us our sins and to cleanse us from all unrighteousness"

(1 John 1:9). Also let us consider the blessings and warning in Proverbs 28: 13,

" He who conceals his transgression. will not prosper, but he who confesses and forsakes them will find compassion".

If we can heed this warning every day in our lives, it will serve us well and keep us from sinning against God and others.

Forthrightness in our dealings with God and the people we sin against is helpful in us receiving forgiveness and living with clear conscience in our lives.

The last strategy to help us overcome temptations is for us to always keep eternal perspective in everything we do.

Ecclesiastes exhorts us to avoid a short-sighted " under the sun" mentally and instead remember what happens in God's eternity: " The conclusion, when all ihas been heard, is fear God and keep His commandments, because this applies to every person. For God will bring every act to judgement, everything whicht is hidden, whether good or evil" (Ecclesiastes 12:13-14).

With this in mind, let us choose rewards over temporal pleasures that is contrary to God's plan for us. These few strategies should help us to avoid the traps of Satan that cause us to sin. Matthew 26:41 encourages us to " Watch and pray so that you will not fall into temptation. The Spirit is willing but the flesh is weak". I also say watch and pray.

CHAPTER 17

How to Grow in Christian Maturity

Every believer needs to grow up in Christ. We call it spiritual maturity or spiritual growth. We all understand the concept of growth in the physical development of humans and we know that it is very important. For example, babies or children are immature physically and mentally but we expect them to develop. If not, there is a problem.

Spiritual growth is a similar concept but far more important for all believers. Growth means development or improvement towards maturity and in the Bible, we call it

" perfection". When we are born again as a child of God, we are spiritually immature. But as time passes on, we should develop qualities and abilities which the Bible says charaterize the mature. For example, a congregation matures as the individual members mature in the Church. Because of this, the Bible lays emphasis on the need to grow and mature spiritually. Here are a few Bible verses to remind and help us grow spiritually.

Ephesians 4:14-15. " Then we will no longer be infants, tossed back and forth by the waves, and blown here and there by every wind of teaching and by the cunning and craftiness of men in their deceitful scheming. Instead, speaking the truth in love, we will in all things grow up into him who is the Head, that is Christ".

2 Peter 3:18 " But grow in the grace and knowledge of our Lord and Savior Jesus Christ".

2 Thessalonians 1:3. " We ought always to thank God for you, brothers, and rightly so, because your faith is growing more and more, and the love everyone of you has for each other is increasing".

Philippians 1:19. " And this is my prayer that your live may abound more and more in knowledge, depth and insight".

If we are not growing up spiritually or maturely, many problems result. Some believers go back to the world, others cause strife because of ignorance or become stumbling blocks because of irregular Church attendance, worldliness, or indifference. Just as children need to do certain activities to grow, so must believers. There are certain steps we need to take if we want to grow into maturity.

The first is to desire to grow. We cannot grow if we don't have the desire to grow. Every child that is born into this world, wants to grow. They can't wait to grow to become independent and do things for themselves. So just as in the physical realm children want to grow, likewise in spiritual matters, believers or born again Christians must want to grow. 1 Peter 2:2 says " Like newborn babies, crave pure spiritual milk, so that by it you may grow up in your salvation".

If we seem to like being babies, we would never want to grow because it is easier to be baby believers than to grow up because we don't want to take responsibility for anything. Others will do everything for us we think. Especially in the Church, we don't have to do anything,

But being a baby Christian is not the goal of life as we all know. We are born babies so we can grow up to be productive and useful. Likewise, we are born again as Christian babies so we can become mature Christians and actively serve the Lord.

The second point is we need spiritual food from God's Word. Just as a child cannot grow physically without proper food, likewise spiritually, we cannot grow without feeding on the Word of God. We have seen in 1 Peter 2:2 how it is important to

"crave pure spiritual milk, so that by it you may grow up in your salvation", so also in 2 Peter 3:18 it says " But grow in the grace and knowledge of our Lord and Savior Jesus Christ". In addition, Matthew 4:4 stresses the same point of feeding on the Word of God: " Jesus answered: It is written: 'Man shall not live by bread alone, but on every word which comes from the mouth of God'. Lastly, Ephesians 4:15 says " Instead, speaking the truth in love, we will in all things grow up into him who is the Head, that is Christ". In all these Bible verses, we see that it is important to feed on the Word of God to grow spiritually.

To get the nourishment we need therefore, we must study the Bible, pray, worship, attend Church meetings and fellowship with each other so we can grow in love, grace and knowledge. In the Book of Hebrew Chapter 5, the Apostles were very disappointed by the slow growth of the Hebrews and brought a word of warning: "Infact, though by this time you ought to be teachers, you need someone to teach you elementary truths of God's word all over again. You need milk not solid food. Anyone who lives on milk, being still an infant, is not acquainted with the teachings of righteousness" (Hebrew 5: 12-13).

In Acts 17:11, the Apostles commended the Berean Jews for their deligence in studying the Word of God: " Now the Berean Jews were of more noble character than those in Thessalonica, for they received the message with great eagerness and examined the Scripture every day to see if what Paul said was true". All these passages tell us the importance of studying the Bible to grow spiritually.

Maybe you have not been serious about Bible Study. You cannot grow into a mature Christian if you neglect reading and studying your Bible. Get at it now if you want to grow spiritually.

The third important factor in spiritual growth is through exercises and practice.

Every actor, athlete and musician knows that exercise and practice is important to improve their skills and that developing skills require continual repetition. We see children practice skills over and over again. We often say practice makes perfect. Well, so are exercise and practice important for spiritual growth. The Book of Hebrews stresses this concept of spiritual exercise and practice:

"But solid food is for the mature, who by contant use have trained themselves to distinguish good from evil". 1 Timothy 4:7 also says "Have nothing to do with godless myths and old wives tales, rather train yourself to be godly". So spiritual growth involves contant study of God's word. To neglect this important exercise and practice is to continue to be a baby Christian.

Lastly, growing into spiritual maturity takes time and patience. We all know that children do not grow instantly. At birth they are so small that we can hold them in our arms easily. But soon they begin to grow gradually to a point we cannot hold them in our arms. As time passes,they grow to become children, youth, young adults and eventually adults. Likewise spiritually, we do not expect to grow overnight. The Bible says much about spiritual growth. In James 1:4 we are told "Perseverance must finish it's work so that you may become mature and complete, not lacking anything".

As new born Christians,we cannot know everything and do everything right away. We must be willing to take our time to study and develop abilities. No one becomes a mature and believer one day. Take your time to grow into maturity by reading your Bible, studying it, praying, fasting and worshipping.These and other Christian exercises are very necessary for spiritual growth.

Don't be discouraged when you make mistakes in your spiritual growth. You are not alone. People like Moses, David, Peter, Paul, Thomas and all the Apostles made mistakes growing up spiritually but through repentance and confession, they became great workers and preachers for Christ". Proverbs 28:1 says "A man who remains stiff-necked after many rebukes will suddenly be destroyed without remedy". What is needed is repentance and patience to learn to do the right thing in our lives. We all need to grow as Christians and we can all grow if we simply apply these Biblical principles for spiritual growth in our lives. May the Lord guide and help us grow to become muture Christian in the name of the Father, Son and the Holy Spirit. Amen.

CHAPTER 18

How to Please God in Your Life

In this Chapter, I want to guide you on how to please God in your life. From my experience, there are many things we can do to please God as we lead our lives and are led by the Holy Spirit. I find obedience and faith in God to be very paramount.

Each time I exercised faith in God and obeyed His command, and followed the guidance of the Holy Spirit, the more blessings I received in my life— blessings of peace, joy, fulfillment, courage in difficult and trying moment in my life and contentment. Nevertheless, there are more things we can do to please God every day according to the Bible. Let us go through some of them.

The first is having faith in God.

" And without faith it is impossible to please God, because anyone who comes to him must believe that he exists and that he rewards those who earnestly seek him" (Hebrews 11:6).

This passage identifies faith as the prerequisite for pleasing God. Faith is belief in God and believing that He will do what He says He will do.

There are many Biblical examples of people who had faith in God listed in Hebrews Chapter 11. Enoch was one. He lived in an increasingly wicked and evil world before the Flood in Noah's time but he didn't go the evil way other people were going. Instead, he " walked with God" and "he pleased God" (Genesis 5:24, and Hebrews 11:5). When we believe in God and believe what he says, that faith will please Him.

The second way to please God is to be spiritually minded. The Bible says "To be carnally minded is death, but to be spiritually minded is life and peace. The carnal mind is enmity against God: for it is not subject to the law of God, nor indeed can be. So then, those who are in the flesh cannot please God" (Romans 8:6-8).

Therefore, the Bible makes it clear that there are two mind sets— the human one which is carnal and the one led by the Spirit of God which is the spiritual mind

(Romans 8:9). So having the Holy Spirit

dwell in us and leading us is another way of pleasing God. I have made it clear earlier that to receive the Holy Spirit and to be led by the Holy Spirit, one needs to repent and confess Jesus Christ as Lord and Savior. In Acts 2:38, this is emphasized:"Repent and let everyone of you be baptized in the name of Jesus Christ for the remission of sins and you shall receive the gift of the Holy Spirit". Being born again, therefore, pleases God. Jesus said there is " joy in heaven over one sinner who repents"(Luke 15:7). Being saved and being spiritually minded, indeed pleases God.

The third way to please God is to fear God. Psalm 147:11 says" The Lord takes pleasure in those who fear Him, in those who hope in His mercy". God does not delight in having us be terrified in Him. What this passage means is that we must fear God not because it is good for Him, but because it's good for us to properly recognize that He is more powerful than anything else. To acknowledge this fact, therefore, shows our deep respect for Him. When we properly fear and respect God, it motivate us to avoid sin as seen in Exodus 20:20 and it will remind us that God will hold us accountable for our sins.

By fearing God, it allows us to rely on Him and revere Him as Omnipotent, Omnipresent and Omniscient.

The fourth way of pleasing God is doing His will. In Hebrews 13:21, we read: (May God) "equip you with everything good for doing His will, and may He work in us what is pleasing to Him, through Jesus Christ, to whom be glory forever and ever. Amen".

Doing God's will means doing His desires, his commands,and his plans as expressed in the Bible. This means we must study the Bible, meditate on it, pray about it in order to understand God and His will. His will for us involves "doing every good work which entails maturing spiritually and becoming more like Him (Matthew 5:48).

Jesus set a good example for us by doing God's will when he faced the cruel beatings and crucifixion for our sins. When he prayed:"" Nevertheless, not my will, but Yours be done in Luke 22:42, He was willing to give himself completely to show His love and to do His Father's will.

We must seek to please God in our lives by asking Him in prayer to help us do His will in our lives.

The fifth way to please God is to obey Him. In 1 Samuel 15:22, we read: " Does the LORD delight in burnt offerings and sacrifices as much as in obeying the voice of the LORD? To obey is better than sacrifice, and to heed is better than the fat of rams". In this passage, Samuel the Prophet, expressed God's displeasure with King Saul who had disobeyed God's direct command with excuse that the people wanted to make sacrifice to God with what should have been destroyed as commanded by God.

Obeying God is absolute. God does not want our gifts if we are going to break his laws to give them. When it comes to obedience to God, He does not command us to obey Him just because it is good for Him, but because it is good for our own good (Deuteronomy 10:13). His laws and commands are beneficial to us. As a result of obeying Him, we grow godly, develop righteous character and become more like Him. This is how we please God and he has promised to bless those who "keep my Sabbath, and choose what pleases me" and who " abstain from sexual immorality" and avoid breaking any of God's commandments (1 Chronicles 28:17, Isaiah 56:4 and 1 Thessalonians 4:1-3).

"To obey is better than sacrifice".

The sixth way to please God is to study and follow the example of Jesus Christ.

During a vision of the future Kingdom of God recorded in Matthews Chapter 17, known as the transfiguration, God impressed on Peter, John and James the preeminence of Jesus Christ. "This is My beloved Son, in whom I am well pleased. Hear Him" (Matthews 17:5). Jesus is truly the Son of God and there is no one who has pleased God more! We should therefore, hear Him and follow His example. Jesus said he always did " those things that please Him" (John 8:29), so we also must study all the Gospels and learn how to please God.

These are some of the few points on how to please God. As you study the Gospels, you will find more ways to please God. May His grace and peace be unto you always in Jesus' name.

CHAPTER 19

How-to Trust God at All Times

In this Chapter of " The Guidance of the Holy Spirit", I want to discuss how you can trust God at all times in your life.

Life is unpredictable and trusting God in all things is part of our spiritual growth.

There are ups and downs along life's pathway and many of us will encounter some challenging circumstances or difficulties. When it comes to trusting God in challenging situations, trials, temptations, sickness, financial difficulty and other issues along the path, it is not easy to trust in God. When times are good, it feels easier to trust God, but when times feels difficult for us, can we still trust God?

The answer is yes. God's unchanging character can give us a firm foundation when things feel unsteady and uncertain in our lives.

Trusting God means to believe in His reliability, truth, ability or strength. Trusting God also means we must trust in His Word. The Bible tells us that God cannot lie, that He always keep His promises, He loves us, and has good plans for us. Trusting in Him means to believe that what He says about Himself, the world, and about us is true. If we trust in God, he is much more reliable than anyone we can trust. When things feel difficult, God does not ask us to keep it to ourselves. 1 Peter 5:7 says "Cast all your anxiety on Him because He cares for you". Psalm 56:8 also says " You keep track of all my sorrows. You have collected all my tears in your bottle. You have recorded each one in your book". God cares about us and loves us. Therefore, we can demonstrate our trust in Him by talking about all our feelings and circumstances with Him through prayer.

When we trust God and life is hard for us, we go to Him and His Word and act in obedience to what He says in His Word.

By doing so, we trust that He will ultimately take care of the rest. There will be no need for us to look for security in any other things if our trust in God is firm.

A good example is Our Lord Jesus Christ.

When he was overwhelmed by what was before Him (the Cross), this is what he told his disciples: "My soul is overwhelmed with sorrow to the point of death", " Stay here and keep watch" (Mark 14:34). And he went straight to God his Father to pray because Jesus knows that God cares for our hurts and pays attention to our needs.

If the God of this universe cares for us and pays attention to us, this should strengthen our trust in Him during times of hardship and the unknown ahead of us.

Let me suggest some practical ways to trust God in our daily life:

First, let us not depend on ourselves in this world. We live in a world where trust must be earned but trust seems to be limited.

Proverbs 3:5 tells us to "Trust in the LORD with all your heart and lean not on your own understanding". This means that even though most of us face disappointments and challenges in life which we have depended on ourselves, the best we can do is to depend on God at all times in all our circumstances. The Bible teaches that the life God has called us to live means we learn to depend on His understanding every day.

We know that God possesses all wisdom but sometimes our trust in Him can be difficult. Therefore each day in our lives, we need to consciously lay aside our plans and expectations and surrender to God's plan for our lives. When I became born again, I learned to depend on God every day in my life. As a result of my trust in Him, I have always found His grace, mercy, love guidance and provision for me in every situation. So, the first step of trusting in God is to depend on God and not on yourself. This must be very consistent in your life.

The second step in trusting God is to surrender to God. Surrendering to God means we must cry out to Him. This begins with our lips and our thoughts. Proverbs 3:6 says " In all your ways acknowledge Him, and he will make your paths straight"

Prayer is very important if we want to depend on God. When we pray, we acknowledge that His ways are better and higher than ours, we show that we are surrendering our troubles, burdens and dreams in this able hands for the Bible says when we reach out to God in prayer, He hears us. " Evening, morning and noon, I cry out of distress, and he hears my voice" (Psalm 55:17). Trusting in God therefore, involves prayer and crying out to God for His help.

The third step in trusting God is to avoid sin and evil. There are so many things in this world that can clutter our relationship with God and cause us not to trust in Him. 1 John 2:16 warns us "For everything in the world— the cravings of sinful man, the lust of his eyes and the boasting of what he has and does– comes not from the Father but from the world". This means our sin can easily become a stumbling block in our relationship with God. Life works better for us if we remember that the true source of blessings is God and focus on the things that please Him.

Proverbs 3:7 says " Do not be wise in your own eyes, fear the LORD and shun evil". The only way to live a life pleasing to God is to "Flee the evil desires of youth, and pursue righteousness, faith, love and peace along with those who call on the Lord out of pure heart" (2 Timothy 2:22). Fleeing the evil desires that pull at us means spending time crying to God and trusting in Him.

God has promised to honor our commitment to Him when we avoid evil. Avoiding evil is not easy but we must make serious change in our lives in order to honor God with our trust.

The fourth step in trusting God is to listen to the Holy Spirit. When the Lord Jesus Christ promised his disciples to send the

Holy Spirit to the Church, he pointed out that this Counselor would be their spiritual guide. "But the Counselor, the Holy Spirit whom the Father will send in my name, will teach you all things and will remind you of everything I have said to you" (John 14:26).

If in our daily lives, we are led by the Holy Spirit, our trust in God will grow as we become obedient to the teachings and guidance of the Holy Spirit.

There are other things we can do to trust in the LORD: They include putting God first in all we do, studying the Word of God and applying His Word in our lives, and knowing that God loves us and is ever prepared to hear us and answer our prayers. We can absolutely trust God always, depend upon on God anytime, and abide in His love forever, God is eternal and awesome. Trust Him in the name of the Father Son and the Holy Spirit. Amen.

CHAPTER 20

The Epilogue

Well, thank you for coming along with me on my life's journey. I hope that by sharing my testimony with you and giving you some teachings on how you can become a better disciple of Jesus Christ and fullfil your life's purpose in Christ has been helpful to you.

My prayer will always be with you. Gather courage and arise and shine in whatever God has called you to do in His name.

May the blessings of Almighty God the Father, Son and the Holy Spirit abide with you now and forever. Amen. Shalom!

www.ingramcontent.com/pod-product-compliance
Lightning Source LLC
LaVergne TN
LVHW091557060526
838200LV00036B/881